AMERICA—
Land of the Rising Sun

by Don Smithana

Published by: ANASAZI Publishing Group
San Diego, CA 92126

AMERICA, Land of the Rising Sun

A Fascinating Revelation that can provide us with an entirely New view of these American nations. Using the Verbal native descriptions of Ancient America, the history of early civilizations of these continents is reconstructed, and a Lost Empire is found, located right in the Heart of North America! Was this Empire, then, Exported to JAPAN?

Published by:
ANASAZI Publishing Group
8190 E. Mira Mesa Blvd. Ste.360
San Diego, California 92126
U.S.A.

AMERICA, Land of The Rising Sun

by Don R. Smithana

CONTENTS

PREFACE
INTRODUCTION

DEDICATION

Wm. J. Smithana
D. M. Smithana

whose pioneering efforts and spirit of conservation along with early recollections inspired a respect for nature and a deep interest in the Americas, as well as the Woodland spirit.

This book is additionally dedicated to the understanding of the early People of the Americas, so that we might also better understand the Americas and the World we live in.

(The Author is appreciative of the support and patience of Ann, Lyn and Robert Smithana over the years of research the project entailed.)

Preface

AMERICA,
LAND of the RISING SUN

An AMAZING New Look at History and the AMERICAS. By generating and using a scientific Language MODEL, a Proposal is introduced that can make the NATIVE INDIAN Languages, for the first time, more understandable!

The North and South AMERICAN Continents appear to have an overlay of a rich, singular Ancient language. It is related to that of early EURO-ASIAN nomads, and, like the reverse of fossilized artifacts, has been preserved for us in a modern form in the islands of JAPAN, as NIHONGO, the Japanese language.

Had these nomadic Tribesmen wandered out of the NEW WORLD of the Americas 15,000 years ago to invade the Asian plains? Were the AMERICAS a "cradle of civilization" for the Cro-Magnon Man? Or as many scholars believe, were the Americas invaded by a hunting/gathering society from ASIA? This is certainly true within the last 2000 years. This is exactly what the AZTEC language tells us, but before this—where does this study and BOLD NEW proposal lead us?

America Without the Smoke and Mirrors

Information covering a thousand years and more of American history is presented in this book. These pages will provide, besides information, a considerable amount of controversy, maybe even disbelief. It is not just a book about America, not just a book about American Indians, nor is it another book about the business relationships between two aggressive economic powers, America and Japan! Perhaps it could be called an **"analytical history"** book.

By whatever name you call it, the topic can be of immense interest to historians as well as modern students of business and civilization, past and present. Much of the information is new.

Some may call it HERESY (Greek definition as heretic—"one who chooses for himself"). It sheds new light on these AMERICAN CONTINENTS, illuminating our common words and ideas with a fresh new perspective. Is there really a need for more study of America and its natives?

It has been facetiously reported that the typical American Indian family consists of "a father, mother, child and an anthropologist". There is no intention here to further complicate—in fact, I believe the overview of our native Americans is much simplified and understandable when related to the world and language with which they lived! A world and language ripped apart by **an inrush of European lifestyle and values so different from their own.**

These pages will show that we have all been looking at this whole New World as if **through a LOOKING GLASS—a distorted reflection of European viewpoints and language.** How much more clear and focused does the image become when we view the Americas directly **from an Asiatic viewpoint** using no mirror at all!

As one Indian chief lamented, "the White man will never understand the Indian because he does not understand America"! Without a doubt, that Native Chief was on the right track. When we understand the rich heritage we call America, then we might better understand and appreciate the peoples who for centuries had called it their homeland.

And by understanding the Americas we will surely also understand better **the Asia we face today as present and potential economic trading partners.**

For both these purposes, this book is written.

What manner of ancient organization gives the agressive image and vitality that American businessmen today see in Japan?

WAS THE CULTURE OF JAPAN "MADE IN THE USA"?

Introduction — America, Land Of The Rising Sun

Over the last several decades, we have come to realize that our World is not very large. And it seems to be getting smaller. The impact of technology has had that effect. The jumbo jets, carrying air freight to all parts of the globe on a one-day schedule, backed up by communications between those same remote locations using satellites and fiber optics, makes it all possible.

We are in a NEW AGE. Just as Columbus was in a new age. He wasn't the first to "discover" America—he just happened to visit it a few years after the printing press was developed. And he worried, it is said, that after returning to Spain, his report to the Queen might be intercepted, printed, and possibly distributed widely before the Spanish Monarchs could be advised. If Lief Ericson's times had had printing presses, it might perhaps have been quite a different history book.

Following closely on World War II has been a technology revolution along with the posturing and elbowing of the great nations of the globe to attain economic growth and influence. The world economic picture has changed drastically in the last 40 years, and emerging as two of the dynamic dominant nations, **are Japan and America (USA).**

They are surprisingly curious bedfellows—a large semi-continent with a myriad of natural resources, and a tiny group of four islands with little more than guts as a resource.

So, it is even more surprising to see the histories of these two great **economic entities interlocked in a manner never before imagined.** It is a rather large and encompassing topic, the beginnings of America, it's culture, and perhaps the beginning of a **whole new Asiatic culture.** For it can be seen that over a thousand years ago a common root language occupied possibly two American continents and part of Asia. It was a language area much larger than the Roman Empire. **This would make it one of the largest language resources on the planet! It seems to be one of the ancient proto-languages.**

I see within probability that our North America was using an archaic language similar to what we now call NIHONGO, or Japanese. This is probably not a new discovery. It has been in some small ways addressed by several amateur anthropologists (see Chap.1). But much of this material is new and certainly controversial. I **believe, in time, it will prove to be in a large part accurate.**

History and learning should be an interesting type of activity, so this is not presented as an academic analysis. Like most studies, they raise more questions than they do answers, and many questions arise from these propositions. Reconstructing an ancient language (unwritten) is an interesting but frustrating task. The benchmark meanings have often been lost to us so that our progress is hard to measure. And with each day that goes by, more **original accurate meanings are taken to the grave by the few remaining users of the language.**

Nevertheless, borrowing from the technique of scientific models, and applying intuitive probability, a picture can be generated to which elements can then be added. The MODEL grows and gets corrected where needed.

The picture is one of an America of natural resources and beauty which became an empire for people of whom we know very little. Can this study help shed light on the early beginnings of this strange (by Western standards) civilization? In several instances you may have to throw away preconceived ideas, but I certainly hope I give you good reason to accept it. For, on a basis of probability, that all these correlations are wrong would make for astronomical odds. Now that a model of American Language has been proposed, it should be easier for historical research to proceed.

This "hypothesis" is one that actually is difficult to accept by many scientists but this would only deter me should I have a position in, say, the field of Anthropology and were in fear of being ridiculed by my peers. My field of Electronics and Computers allows me independent insight to the history of our continent and nation. And, of course, we are reminded that the first concept of Continental drift was proposed **not by a geologist,** but a meteorologist—and the theory took 50 years to be finally confirmed and accepted by the professional community.

The Americas have been for a long time a set of continents presenting a mysterious and cloudy view of their history. It appears that the Native American Indians are like characters written into a narrative of which the beginning is unclear and the end is yet unseen.

It is distressing that we in the United States have 26 states using Indian names, most of which I feel have not been properly translated. It is a rich and amazing history which has been either re-discovered or uncovered for the first time! I say "re-discovered" because there are linguistic hints that the original meanings first encountered by European explorers may have accurately existed, but were lost to both the immigrant and the Indian in the confusion, conflict, and hyper-activity of settling a new nation.

My work is not that of a linguist. It might be classified more as "geolinguistics" defined by Mario Pei (An Invitation to Linguistics) as:

".........the practical present day application of linguistic science; in the same sense that engineering is the practical application of the laws of physics."

"..........geolinguistics is of interest to everybody who has any occasion whatsoever to travel abroad, establish foreign contacts, or be concerned with the state of the world."

"........the function of the geolinguist is to present the world's languages in PROPER PERSPECTIVE, — and to describe their relative

importance and usefulness in various connec-
tions."

NOTE:

The scope of this work covers a couple
thousand years and such diverse and dynamic
people that it is difficult to keep a continuous
story-line.

For the reader who may wish to browse various
chapters of particular geographic interest, at times
basic information is restated. This provides to a
limited degree, chapters with stand-alone
capability for this type of reader.

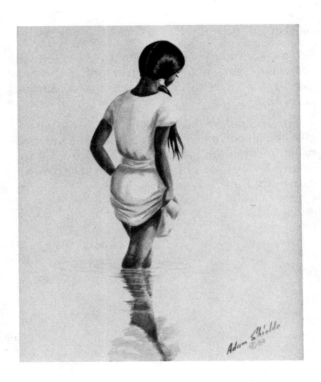

Fig. 1.1

A NEW UNDERSTANDING OF AMERICA REFLECTED
BY THE ARCHAIC WORDS OF AN ASIATIC LANGUAGE.

1. *The Amazing American History— A New View*

The words were uttered by an American Indian Chief, Luther Standing Bear, early in this century, **"The White man does not understand the American Indian for the reason that he does not understand America!"**.[1] How true this observation has been, and to this day still represents an overwhelming substance of truth. We have here a great land reshaped and rebuilt to the needs of the European settler. Yet only a few dwell along the road to the future to reflect upon and study the greatness this land once was, and still is. **Twenty-six** American States have Indian names for which the translations are inadequate or unknown.

A Global Village

It was early in the first half of this century that an explosive growth in technology allowed most of us to realize that we all lived in a global village. Communications, transportation, and information were the keys to opening up the planet to either benevolent trade or frivolous power plays. Before mid 1900 the Earth was figuratively shrinking each month that passed; one could hear the voices of world economic power, each demanding elbow room. They resulted from intensive Com-

1

munications, Transportation, and Information. To a large extent, electronics led this reformation. The world continued to shrink. Measuring the continents in Time, the telephone and jet airplane reduced the furtherest empire to minutes or hours. Satellite radio repeaters and cargo jet planes fulfilled the necessary ingredients of world trade—immediate information and timely inventory control.

In a parallel activity to these new concepts, there began a calculated growth in a small Pacific entity, the Islands of the Japanese Empire. In retrospect, this is not a surprise. America, through the rich natural resources of geography, geology, and sociology had emerged as a powerful surviving entity in the world community. And another world player, Japan, would soon be on the technical and economic scene, a player that many thought had been left sitting on the bench.

But it was fairly obvious that this was an island power soon to be acknowledged, for it seemed to be born of the same stuff as America. Perseverance, toil, innovation, and adventure was what put the **hardy American pioneer into the wide picture** of American woodland, desert and mountains. Add to this, the ingredients of some of our oppressed immigrants, that of patience and self-discipline and **you have the equation for a New Japan**.

But can we find an even more amazing similarity between these two modern economic giants straddling the legendary Pacific Rim? **The answer is "YES"**, and amazing and unbelievable might be added to this startling revelation. For these two countries, so apparently far apart in current culture and geography, have a common background somehow **exposed in a similar language.** The language of the Americas show a very close correlation to that spoken in ancient and modern Japan.

While many cultures of the world also are in many ways similar, these two cultures and ancient nations, in particular, also show a surprising congruence never before identified or revealed.

That is the subject of this book.

THE TIME HAS COME, the WALRUS SAID...

A young American soldier was in the Philippines guarding a trainload of Japanese military prisoners bound for a temporary Army camp until they could be repatriated. It was the closing days of World War II, just north of Manila. It could have been like many other incidents of that period except for one difference. **The American soldier was a Native American Indian,** called "Chief" by his comrades in arms.

One of the Japanese prisoners overheard this nickname and approached the American guard, Mani Boyd, a Menominee from Wisconsin. He had been raised from boyhood in traditional Indian manner and culture, (as best possible in modern times). The Japanese re-patriate, upon seeing the guard raising his weapon, cautioned him not to be alarmed — he only wanted to talk with him and discuss his thoughts with a native American Indian for the first time. He had studied at the

3

University in Manila before the war, and had been recalled to Japan to be drafted into the Army. His English was quite good.

Explaining this to Boyd, he continued that his studies of America had led him to believe that a very strong relationship must have existed between Japanese culture and American Indians. He continued his discussion with Boyd, asking if he might pursue with him the apparent similarities in culture that they may have both shared. He asked how the American Indian buried their dead—was it with the head facing West, toward paradise? Did they have Holy Fires? Indeed, after much detailed questioning the Japanese walked away saying that he was finally satisfied that **"either the American natives came from Japan, or the Japanese arrived from America."**

However, he was not the first to notice this, for during the war years each day brought news of the Pacific theatre of war to the cities and villages of Wisconsin as well as America. Newspaper headlines thrust out with names of Japanese islands and locations that seemed to many who lived in Wisconsin to be quite similar to the Indian names they had become familiar with. Many, but not all, brushed this aside as being coincidental.

I, for one, pursued it when time permitted several months later serving duty during the post-war Occupation of Japan. Could there be a more specific connection? I was encouraged in my studies in Yokohama by an American girl from Cleveland. Her name was Natsue and she had lived in the Yokohama area during the war as a prisoner. She had been given a high school graduation present of a visit to her grandparents in Tokyo in November, 1941. As a result, caught in the war, she was forced to spend the years in Japan under arrest. She was quite fluent in both English and Japanese and encouraged Americans while in Japan to study the intricate culture of the islands.

Based on my studies starting shortly thereafter in Yokohama, the Japanese soldier probably did not realize fully how accurate a conclusion he had made! While Boyd today is retired, his family is helping teach young American natives some of their rich language heritage at the Reservation High School. Where that **amateur Japanese Anthropologist** is today, no one knows but he **was neither first nor alone in his assessment.**

Today, we are looking at the American continents as if through a looking glass — we see an image that is almost clear, but not understandable. What we see is not exactly what is there. And we have been asked to accept what we see even if it makes little sense!

A Language Puzzle Spread
Over 3 Continents

Many people have asked, if the Indian language is related to an Asiatic one, why is it that after centuries of study, no one has identified it? Three reasons come forward: Convenience, Context and Competence in Asiatic language.

✦ **For Convenience,** rather than study old forms of possible Asiatic language links, it is much easier for the American investigator to start off

5

directly with the study of present day Indian language. As many as 600-800 different dialects and variations have been reported. Much of this has been generated within the last 500 years or corrupted by dialects within the language family. This is much like starting out to study the Atomic Structure of silicon with a cup full of gravel.

In fact, dialects are reported to have been nurtured and propagated in both the English and Japanese languages to **serve a provincial purpose of security and isolation.** It was common for people of England and Japan to effect certain pronunciations and descriptions among their groups to more readily identify the outsiders who might be spies or otherwise intruders. To some extent this habit is reported to have resulted in the Cockney English accent as well as the Kansai accents of Western Japan. Even today, as parents, many are aware of their teen age children using similar techniques to confuse and misdirect their parents in either devious or inocuous ways. Black "jive talk" is one example.

The scholar that tries to equate similar meanings can find a host of words that represent the meanings — particularly in family life where girl, woman, mother, sister might be implied by a relationship, not directly. For instance, eldest sister is referred to indirectly as "first born female". Without a "Rosetta Stone"[2] a student could wander for years in such a quagmire to reconstruct a proto-language. In our study, such a Language Rosetta Stone has been developed and is used.

✦ **The CONTEXT** in which a primitive language is used can be very important as explained by Jiri Jelinek of the University of Sheffield.[3] The probable life-style of the speaker and his environment can help one choose from several possible constructions. The Indian, as in any High-Context society, had different meanings for similar sounds. The actual meaning was apparent from context. Thus, knowing the nature of the early native Americans, their interest in abundant food and clear water, their abiding faith in great natural spirits, and an "esprit de corp" to inspire their lives and family relations one can statistically make a selection from several possible word meanings.

For instance, in Wisconsin the early name for the river entering Lake Michigan at Racine was MUSKELLUNGE River (later named ROOT). The language model translates this to MASU KURU ONGE, or "Fish (trout) return with obligation (all at same time)" or are spawning. It also became, erroneously, the name for a Wisconsin sporting fish. Canada also has a river named COULLONGE. The large spawning-runs up the rivers around Lake Michigan are famous even today, drawing the avid fisherman from all over the midwest. These spawning runs were evident as well on both ocean coasts. Without the complexity of weaving a net or fashioning a thin fishing line, spawning fish could be easily caught. The periodic return of fish for these huge spawning-runs from which ample quantities could be easily speared or netted was of immense importance to a fishing/hunting society. The verbal Indian language across America abounds with colorful descriptions of migrating game.

✦ **RESEARCH COMPETENCE in archaic forms of Asiatic language** seems to be a severe shortfall among most of the scholars on American Indians — even those professors who specialize in linguistics. Very few of the various anthropology experts on Indians I have talked with are familiar with Asiatic language—some cite the studies of the **Chinese scholar, Dr. LI among the Athabascan Indians**[4] in 1926 as an exploration of Asiatic possibilities that proved futile.

I feel that **Dr. Li indeed did uncover a link to early Japanese** which somehow was overlooked[5]. While he reported himself to be fluent in Chinese, Japanese and English, it is hard to understand what happened. However, it does seem that fluency in the modern languages can be a deterrent to logical observation. For instance, I asked a friend of mine who had arrived in America from Japan only a year before to comment on the possibility of MICHI-GAN meaning the "Pathway of the Wild Goose". No, he countered, it must have a possessive conjunction added and inverted to **GAN-NO-MICHI (Goose's Path)** which would be grammatically correct! He did not take into account that a thousand years can change ancient grammar.

The above observations are not made in a critical vein, but to in some way answer the valid and **usual question of why haven't these more obvious relationships been previously reported.** In the words of Dr. Yoshida, a prominent linguist researcher in Japan,[6] he advised that "this theory will certainly surprise and inform Japanese scholars who never thought of such a method of comparative studies of languages relating to the American Indians."

Are there several underlying cultures beneath this overlay of Algonquin or proto-Japanese culture? Using this as a starting point, will the ancient languages of India, Sumeria, Africa, Indonesia, and China also be found in the Americas? One scholar reports a close similarity of some American Indian languages to those of Africa and the Middle East! One eminent Arabic scholar, upon hearing my proposal remarked with amazement that his perusal of an Arabic-Japanese dictionary revealed so many similarities. Was this the original source of the "Language of the Americas"? Did it come from North Africa and then proceed across these American continents to Alaska and the Japanese islands where it became refined into the Japanese language (NIHONGO) of today?[7] My proposal of this AMERICAN Language ROSETTA STONE will certainly help students familiar with those other languages to focus on suspected correlations.

---

[1] *"Touch the Earth"*; T.C. McLuhan, Promentory Press

[2] *Developed in Chapter 4*

[3] *Classical Japanese/English Grammar dictionary, by Jelinek, 1976 Univ. of Sheffield Press*

[4] *"Introduction to Historical Linguistics" by Anthony Arlotta*

[5] *See Chap. 10*

[6] *Mr. Yoshida, Linguist and Editor of Japan Petrograph Society Journal.*

[7]*The other direction, from Asia and the islands of Japan to all of the Americas is an interesting and popular alternative. The probability of such a small island area so close to China to develop an independent language, and then propagate into such wide, diverse, and inhospitable places from the Amazonians to the Eskimos seems low. Why are the Chinese and Japanese languages so different? Will the Japanese language, in addition to being related to the America language, also have a relation to Sumerian and ancient Canaanites (Phoenicia)? If so, from which direction did it enter the islands of Japan. The ancient names for Japan will be developed later, adding some insight to this question.*

FIG. 2.2

AMERICA, THE MYTHICAL LAND
OF PERPETUAL YOUTH

2. *America, Land of Fu Sang*

Looking back through thousands of years of unwritten language can be like looking through a fog, a fog so dense that light can hardly pierce it. However, by reconstructing the language heritage left to us by the Native American Indians, we have an excellent chance to study that which predates written history. Just as Radar extends our visual limits, we can use new techniques to pierce the linguistic fog enshrouding our Americas. It will reveal an interesting and intriguing concept of our Americas never before offered by historians.

Researchers in the Physical Sciences have long ago developed **methods to deal with understanding in more detail those items that are too small or remote to be directly observed.** Electronic and Atomic engineers have long worked with forces unseen, particles too small to even imagine, and yet have set up models and mathematical equations with which these forces and particles can be compared, predicted, and "understood". Not that our understanding is complete or final, but the models so well fit what we observe that we can actually predict behaviour with "RULES" set down for us by such great people as Maxwell, Copernicus, Keppler, Newton, Einstein, Descartes and Leibnitz.

Can the METHODOLOGY of this kind of scientific thinking be extended into the social scientists arena where probability can be used to derive an overwhelming language correspondence, the proof of which has eluded the student of Linguistics for centuries?

I believe it can. The unwritten languages of the natives of the great continents of North and South America provide a challenge of immense proportions. It is only when the culture of such societies is considered that it becomes easier to reconstruct an immensely rich language heritage to which we have become the beneficiaries.

Just as the ROSETTA STONE discovered in 1799 provided a starting place to unravel some of the most complex written language of the Mediterranean area, so do I feel that this work might form a primitive model upon which can be built a much clearer understanding of our American heritage.

And we will be in a position to form a much clearer perspective on another perplexing and to Western eyes enigmatic society, namely that of the **Japanese Empire.** For such a small geographic entity to become such a powerful force in technology and economics surely must represent a cultural foundation much different from most other societies. **As we probe inside the dynamic, seething nucleus of the "cultural molecule" we call JAPAN, we see the possiblity of an "atomic" makeup every bit as complex and powerful** as the neutrinos, protons, and electrons envisioned in the atom by Nels Bohr.

WHERE did this Power of the People, this Energy come from?

Was It "Made In America" ?

We should not overlook the strong possiblity that "American civilizations" have contributed a large part to this Asiatic Empire. For it appears that a thousand years ago, a language quite similar to JAPANESE was one of the most widespread on the face of the planet EARTH. It may have encompassed the largest landmass made up of the two huge American continents, as well as the tiny Japanese islands off China's coast. It seems to have spread over northern Euroasia as well. Nihongo, the Japanese language today appears to be the modern remains of that fossilized proto-language which was shared by such a large area of the earth.

A Garden of Eden

Was our land a veritable "Garden of Eden" where abundance was the norm? Did the country have a "Fountain of Youth" where people stayed young "forever".? Just over three hundred years ago, when upbraiding the White man for his senseless forays upon the countryside, one Indian chief (Gaspesian, 1676) told them that they had brought hunger and disease to the Indian community—where once his people lived to 130 or 140, they could no longer expect such life.[1] Was he exaggerating?

Irish legend said the land was TIR NA nOG, and it was the land of the young but you had to sail West to find it.[2] **Was this land also known in ASIA for the same longevity?** In China the myth also continued that you could travel East a 'long distance' to reach the land of FU SANG where you could enjoy long life. An ancient engraved stone by Monks at the Chinese Santung province proclaims this "myth" and also advises the potential traveler to take along many young boys and girls because the trip will be long, and his own youth will be exhausted before arrival. Was this distant land JAPAN (as some thought) or were the ancient Monks describing the AMERICAS?

Had other early Chinese explorers made the COLUMBUS MISTAKE in reverse; setting about to find mythical America (Land of the "big sheep" buffalo), they intercepted Japan before they found the Americas?

Was there a measure of truth to the mythology, about the Fountain of Youth, sought after in vain by Ponce de Leon in Florida? Was it the Americas which through European and Asian isolation had been free of some of the worlds most dreadful plagues and diseases? And had the reputation spread to early Irish and Chinese civilizations by nomads leaving the Americas? Early Chinese writings reveal stories of these fabled lands and pyramids by travelers who must certainly have been describing ancient Meso-American Empires. And it can be shown here that these Empires and language were even brought to ASIA by the travelers to be installed into the islands we now call JAPAN.[3]

16

My proposal was offered to one outstanding Midwestern Anthropologist. It was termed new and "controversial" but with the encouraging thought to "keep up the work against all odds, if possible". So many of the professors are reluctant to even consider such a new perspective. Some see no need nor have the time to even review its overwhelming evidence.

Many feel and express the thought that re-constructing an ancient language in this manner is impossible. I certainly feel they are wrong. Some, unfortunately, appear to lack enthusiasm which comes close to apathy. Or is it that they feel threatened to enter an area of Asiatic archaic **language for which they feel un-trained and ill-adapted?**

Having come from the industry of electronics, I feel the people with "acquired wisdom" of that industry are somewhat more flexible to **acceptance of new perspectives.** After all, in the last few decades they have seen the impossible happen. They have seen development of transistors made from little more than a grain of sand, superconductors made of ceramics, fibers of glass for communications, fist-size computers, and a host of products which were "impossible" just years before.

The use of a model language theory to study the interfacing of New World social elements seems altogether fitting and proper to me, just as the model in physical sciences is a necesary (even if primitive) starting point. At the beginning of my research it seemed that the amazing similarities (see Chap. 12) developed by this model were only

17

a coincidence or perhaps the result of "word borrowing" often seen between parallel cultures.

As more of these instances arose, it became obvious that **this was not coincidence—there is a definite pattern of similar sound useage** between much of American Indian vocabulary and that of present day Japanese language! From this it was only natural to look further back, into archaic language of Japanese.

And finally it appeared that we could predict in some instances what the Indian word would mean if we could find the sound in current or old Japanese. This, it appeared, was possible to do in instances such as described for the words Eskimo and Alaska and Ishpeming.[4]

The use of this Model Language of Americas resulted in such a startlingly clearer view of these civilizations that it was felt it might be made as a proposal upon which to build. Further work might resolve more of the mis-understandings we have lived with.

---

[1] *Touch the Earth, McLuhan pg.49*

[2] *National Geographic Apr. 1976 pg. 576*

[3] *Chap.14*

[4] *Chap.10, 7; It is of interest to note that an obsolete term for "stonewall house" is ISHIBEI MINKI (Ishpeming). The more modern term for "stonewall" is ISHIKABI.*

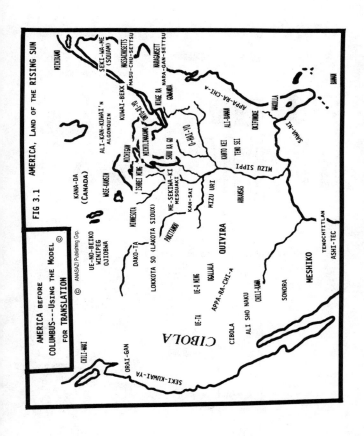

FIG 3.1   AMERICA, LAND OF THE RISING SUN

AMERICA BEFORE COLUMBUS---USING THE MODEL FOR TRANSLATION

© ANASAZI Publishing Grp.

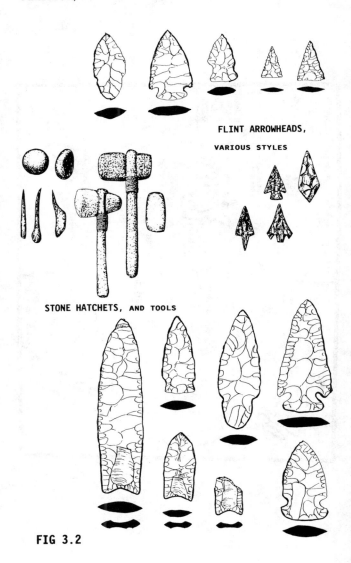

FLINT ARROWHEADS,
VARIOUS STYLES

STONE HATCHETS, AND TOOLS

FIG 3.2

3. Columbus Finds Japan and the Cannibals

What every school student knows is that the quest for a new route to the Far East was the goal of Columbus and many others of that period. Oddly, while records show that China or India was his goal of discovery, he actually was quite confident that he had found JAPAN and a new route to the Orient. This is important for he knew that Chinese shores lay just beyond Japan. The Caribbean islands were surely just off the mainland coast of China. That would make them CIPANGO, the Japanese islands. **We can now, for the first time see the overpowering logic** of this concept and its development.

In Europe, the traders had a large interest in the products of China and Japan, and ostensibly spices and silk were of particular interest. The caravan routes from Europe to China were referred to as the "SILK ROAD" from before biblical times. The biblical Canaanites were called by the Greeks, Phoenicians — but in an Akkadian languge the Phoenicians were known as KINANU [1], with the assumption that it referred to their purple-red dyed clothing. Or was it referring to them as KINU, meaning not color but garments of silk in Japanese?

Because trade routes through the Middle East were well travelled by the caravans, much information about the Far East trickled back to the Europeans. Many of these stories must have sounded like suspicious hear-say to the traders, much as the myths of darkest Africa persevered in European society—stories of people with two heads, or people with tails. It is little wonder then that Europeans did not know where to put their trust. Merchants came back with stories of the fantastic islands off of China, lands of immense riches which were known to them as CIPANGO (JIPANGO), now contracted and spelled as JAPAN.

Knowing from earlier reports of Marco Polo (1298) that the trade routes through India and China also included the legendary islands off the Asia coast called Cipango, Columbus actually thought he had arrived in the islands of Japan! While he named his original area of the Caribbean as ESPANOLA, his maps showed an island as being named CIPANGO. **Was this such a gross mistake**, or was it a wholly understandable error? After his fifth trip to the New World Columbus became ill and died in 1506. **History would record that he died believing that he had actually found the islands of Japan off the main coast of the "India/Chinese nation".** What makes this utterly fantastic is that his presumption may have been enhanced by the natives use of language quite similar to Japanese!

Whatever the misconception, it was still strong enough over a hundred years later (1673) when Father Marquette and Joliet set out on the St. Lawrence river to explore the Great Lakes. They were reported to have anticipated Oriental natives[2] and they had carried with them and wore impressive robes of Chinese style silk when they attended their first meeting with the Ojibwa chiefs. To what extent the natives were impressed has not been recorded.

The island natives encountered by Columbus on his first trip to the New World were quite timid. He reported back to the Queen of Spain that they ran naked around the beaches, hid from them at first and later became more approachable. Their apprehension for these new European visitors was explained later—they were regularly victimized by a marauding group of Indians who captured these peaceful people and ate them. **They called these cannibals the CARIB (Indians).** Today, in Spanish dictionaries, CARIB means "Cannibal" based on these descriptions. In fact, the entire area off the coasts of Meso and South America have come to be called the "CARIBBEAN", a peaceful and romantic name that belies the violence and human beastliness of its source. But where did the name come from? Let us propose a further look!

Columbus must have had a strong reason to make the assumption that he had found the outer islands of Japan. Did he have crew members from Asia that were familiar with the Japanese language that contributed to his erroneous assessment? Yes, as we will see later. For based on this language model, even these remote islands were part of the "Empire of American Rising Sun". At the center of the empire was the area called ALABAMA which translates "To be the entire nation". Out off the Florida coast are the islands called BAMA (spelled today "BAHAMA"). The island distance was readily accessible by large canoes.

These islands then, would also mean part of the "empire". And the model derived word for "hunt" is "CARI" while a "Hunting ground" is "CARIBE". The CARIBBEAN[3] then would be derisively called "The Hunting Ground", a grisly name for a grisly ritual. It was perhaps a religious performance that the CARIB Indians were pursuing in their cannibalistic habit rather than a source of protein. It is easy to see, however, how many of these islands might have had their food animals annihilated by over-hunting.

And since this **same language spread over Canada's provinces**, we might without too much digression also relate these words to the migrating "CARIBOU" which in its abundance would provide food and clothing for the hunters of the North.

The Indians of the North **called these animals CARIBOU**. While these animals were prime hunting targets, that is NOT how their name was derived. The Indians surprisingly said it meant "Hunter". Not because it was hunted, but because of its unique ability to survive icy winters where the food was covered by layers of frozen snow and ice. The Indians perceived that the hooves of the Caribou and Musk Ox are sharp and (unlike deer and buffalo) can more easily cut away the icy glaze covering the winter grasslands to survive in the far north. It was **this food "hunting" ability** that gave them their **Indian name, CARIBOU** (KARI BU—a group that hunts).

Sadly, if we now look at the details of what people and language Columbus found in the New World, **we might also come to realize after 500 years that, soon after he died, history would point out his failures in the discovery of Japan** and the Orient. The doubts he must have harbored would come back and he would bear the mark of failure. But today his judgement might prove to have been more accurate than he has ever been given credit (Fig 3.1).

He had found the doorstep to a rich continent of spices and gold, a land where an early, archaic version of the Japanese language was being used, and the **extended boundary of "an Empire of the Rising Sun"** was located as we shall see later, in the heart of the Mississippi Valley. An empire that had been decimated or soon would be by combined forces of disease and mystery. And how much of this destruction is due to the Europeans may still be the subject of heated discussion.

Hints of this great calamity can be glimpsed later in linguistics. A self-proclaimed Empire spread over thousands of kilometers of the continent and **was held together by a new technology.**

The technology was proclaimed to be, as it was similarly claimed by the Samurai of Japan, the "POWER OF THE BOW AND ARROW". Not only the power of the old fashioned stone-head or obsidian arrow, but power derived from the technology that many years later is described by such anthropological/Indian terms as "CLOVIS MAN" and "QUIVIRA" and "ALGONQUIN". It was the development of the razor sharp FLINT stone arrowhead. The cystal structure of flint allowed flaking and fluting which resulted in an ideal arrowhead before the introduction of steel (Fig. 3.2). It would prove later to be a technology that was more than a match for the muzzle loading pistol at 25 yards. Not until the introduction of the rifle and cannon by the Europeans did this unique technology become overpowered.

How could a skilled mariner such as Columbus have mistaken this new land as being part of the Japanese (CIPANGO) islands? Reports by Columbus biographers reveal that he had the foresight to enlist on his first trip a translator. In anticipation of landing on Oriental shores, **this man was an Arabic/Hebrew trader** who it was thought would be familiar with Oriental language. Indeed, he must have had a keen capability for which, until now, perhaps **he never received credit**. Study indicates that if he had any familiarity with the language of CIPANGO he must certainly have been able to identify it as similar to these islands.

Espanola (later corrupted to Hispaniola) became a marshalling area for Spanish military forays onto the new continents. Within 50 years much of the new World had been assessed, and the Spanish zeroed in on the wealthy empires of Meso-America. North America was slowly developed for its trade in animal skins which brought many of the French adventurers. The English and Dutch came generally as colonists. The point is, very few came as historians, to document the anthropology of this new continent and the enigma of its complex and strange people.

Strange, that is, speaking of course from the viewpoint of Occidental civilization.

Much later, one of the governors of the Michigan territory **learned of the rich folklore of these northern tribal families and ordered his outpost people to write it down wherever it was encountered** so that it might not be lost to posterity. It had been an erroneous assumption by many who had listened to reports by adventurers that these wild lands were populated by savages. Information was so lacking, that when Lewis and Clark were commissioned to make their trip to the Pacific across the Northern route, they were directed by the government to take notes of all the animals, plants, and people they met along the way. Their journal is rich in its description of these important and skillful observations. And this was as late as 1803, 250 years after Coronados expedition to Kansas from Mexico!

We are still close to the American frontier, less than 200 years separates us from these pioneer excursions. It is important that we get the record straight now before more misunderstanding and confusion results. Many perplexing questions seem to be answered clearly when one looks at these American countries from an Asian instead of an European viewpoint! Asia is now using a similar language to that of many of the ancient Indians; it is, however, just a bit more sophisticated.

---

[1] *National Geographic , Aug. 1974-"The Phoenicians, Sea Lords of Antiquity".*

[2] *"Memoirs of Rev. R. Fish Cadle (1796-1857) in the early territories of Michigan & Wisconsin, 1936—by Howard Greene*

[3] *CARRIBBEAN, N ending is specificity just as in Japan today. KARI is hunting for food, while ASSA seems to also be "searching", for food or otherwise. The American Indian had the "th" sound as well as "L" which are no longer used in Japan. Thus, it appears that ASSA KANA BA (ESCANABA) would translate to "Searching place for metal"(Copper and Iron-rich Michigan upper peninsula). Students of language might easily find examples of replacing the letter L with R called RHOTACISM, well known in Japanese language. When clarified, the syllabic division of the American Indian seems identical to the Meso-American Mayan, Inca and Aztec languages, a Consonant-Vowel (C-V) rhythm pattern. This pattern is reported similar in the langue of Italian, Spanish, Japanese and Indonesian.*

FIG 4.1

The Rosetta Stone, discovered in 1799, was the key to deciphering the hieroglyphics that had been incomprehensible for centuries.

4. Generating a Model – Finding a Rosetta Stone

Several years ago while working and studying in Japan I had noticed the similarities between the natural interests of the Native American Indians and those of ancient Japan. Their gardens and sacred grounds were manicured with the care reserved for a deity, and ancestral respect (you might say worship) was a way of life that seemed both thoughtful and natural. It might be considered quite similar to the American Way if one looked beneath the shallow European veneer that had encrusted the Americas during their rapid reformation after the 1500's. While the American native cultural interests seemed quite similar, why were also **many aspects of the Japanese language similar to that of the North American Indian natives?**

Four of the American rivers (two of the largest) had the sound of "Water" in Japanese (MIZU/MISSI). Was this just a coincidence? And an earlier form for water, MINNE appeared in Indian legend as a waterfall, which was near the source of the Mississippi river. It was named Minnehaha, a singular coincidence because combining it with the HAHA (a very unique phrase) gave one "MOTHER of WATERS". The four great rivers were named MISSISSIPPI, MISSOURI, MISSIS-

SAUGA and KALA-MISU (KALAMAZOO). In fact the two early versions of the meanings of KALAMAZOO were "Looking glass water" and "Wild Windy Water" according to native reports. How could such diverse definitions of the river be made by the Indians? Was it just a sound-alike misunderstanding? These both would sound similar today in Japanese as "KAGAMI MIZU" and "KAZE MIZU" respectively. (see Chap. 12). Of course while the "L" sound seemed to exist in the Indian language, it has now disappeared in the present day Japanese (Nihongo).

Hiawatha Wore a Kimono

Indian Legend placed the mother of Hiawatha[1] as WINONA, the eldest daughter of NOKOMIS. In fact, WINONA was the Indian word meaning "eldest sister" which is exactly what it means in early Japanese "first born female" which is "UE NO ONNA" (superior female, but not a current form; see Fig. 15.1).

The legend placed Hiawatha on the shores of Gitchee Gumi, a catchy and poetic sounding place. Historians identify it as the shores of the giant Lake Superior. Coincidentally, UMI today is used as meaning "ocean or inland sea" by the Japanese, and also by the Eskimos.

Early French explorers learned of a popular place along an important river of the west called OUCHITA. We will later see the reason for its outstanding fame and importance (Ch.6). The English would later name it WICHITA. Among early Indian definitions of OUCHITA were "houses in a meadow" which as "UCHI TA" is still a viable but unorthodox Japanese construction meaning "houses in a field".

We do know without a doubt the often major changes made by the white man to the Indian words. The OJIBWA Indians became better known to the settlers as the CHIPPEWA group. This clearly shows the vast reconstruction of the vocabulary necessary before any attempt to trace these archaic word forms into today's modern Japanese vocabulary. This name, OJIBWA, according to the Scotsman GREY OWL, who lived and married among them, meant "Blood Brothers". By todays research, this group would be known as the UJIBUWA (a group of the Clan of Blood Brothers). In Japan, today, the historical SAMURAI warriors are known as the UJI (Blood Brothers Clan)!

But an astounding fact comes to light, proposed by Dr. Yoshida, a leading Japanese linguist and editor. The Japanese use of UJI may have started around feudal times, near 700 AD. Its derivation is thought to be from an earlier expression OJI-OBWA which means "UNCLE/AUNT" or more generally "a society of blood relations". So THIS APPEARS TO BE HOW THE OJIBWA NAME IS DERIVED!

This is even more interesting as we look at the very primitive society in South America known as the YANOMOMO. They run naked in the jungle, with little technology except for the bow and arrow. Their blood-relation society was based on their "Family" defined as an Aunt/ Uncle society! It was also a society based on the value of their important food-source, the Peach-fruit tree. Oddly enough, in Japanese YANOMOMO translates closely to "PEACH FRUIT". Some anthropologists will dismiss these facts as being happenstance, just the luck as in a roll of the dice.

Based on general theory and similarities shown above a **model of the American Indian language** (particularly the Midwest) can be generated. The Northern parts of America were studied to initiate the language model for several reasons:

➤ The early exploration was done by the French who were there primarily for trade, were assimilated into the culture and the conflict over land was minimal. These early French versions of the Indian language appear to be more faithful than later ones that became "anglicized".

➤ The Southern parts of America and Mexico had been dominated by the Portuguese and Spanish. They had a heavy orientation from the missionary groups that accompanied the explorers or followed soon after. Early missionary language schools had their own translation of sounds which for the most part today are not recognized by lay people. It is sometimes difficult to extract the original sound. (Such as CHOMPON [a noodle from southern Japan] for the missionary phonetic TYAMPON).

➤ There seems to be recent movement (linguistically) between Asia and Mid-America such that the language use in this section of America appears more "modern" than other places. "Modern" may be 900-1100 A.D. In Canada, the province of Manitoba uses the current Japanese form of "Place" as BA instead of the earlier more prevalent "RA". It is "The Place of the Manitou spirit".

A Rosetta Stone

The ancient stone found in 1799 near the village of Rosetta in Egypt helped reveal the mysteries of the Egyptian civilization as they appeared in ancient writings. Found by Napoleons soldiers, this stone was a vital key to unraveling the ancient writings and was the most important singular item that provided modern historians with this capability. The stone contained a written story which was presented in three languages, Egyptian hieroglyphics and Egyptian demotic writing along with the Greek translation. Deciphering the Egyptian hieroglyphics was finally possible by the use of this stone.

A "Model" Replaces the Rosetta Stone

The American Indian lived in a "High context society" much as the modern Japanese do. You can see this in both languages, where many parts of speech are often omitted, being implied and understood by both parties. **Groups that are homogenous and closely interactive can operate in this manner** for the actual understanding can be gained from context. The pronoun "You" for instance can be singular or plural in America, except for the old South, where plural becomes "youall". Some confusion might result from the declaration "go hunting" but ordinarily from the context one can discover if it is "I go hunting" or "You go hunting". Just as in English, words like FISH can be singular or plural, verb or noun.

With the "language model" as a modern day ROSETTA STONE, it becomes just a time-consuming task to research the original American Indian words and through "context" establish their most probable original meanings. What makes it a little easier is that in many cases only the most important (to the Indians) words and place-names have been preserved for us. These are words of spiritual significance as well as those for rich sources of food and clear water. (Chapter 12 shows further refinement of the language model). New additions and corrections are made to the model and it grows until it is strong enough to support a more specific theory of where and when the language became related to that modern version we now see on the Japanese islands.

What Was Important to the American Natives?

One has to project himself back in time, and develop a feeling for what the Indians of America and Mexico found important whether they were wandering nomads or permanently settled in a village. Linguistically, this appears to be clear water, abundant food, and a spiritual ease of natural co-existence. They did not want to conquer nature, they wished only to live with the spirit of "Mother Earth" which they called MANITOU. Food in abundance was provided to them by this spirit of the good earth, and it was documented by the Indians as seasons of migrations, both of fish and fowl. The migratory habits of these animals provided simple abundance and their habits left their mark on America in our Indian names of states and rivers! (see glossary, Ch. 12)

But perhaps the most important thing I see from the original Indian languages is the consuming interest in sources of fresh, clear water. This was of even more interest as the American plains opened up beyond the rivers which had provided drinkable water (POTAWATOMI). In searching for fruits and nuts at places known as "ELMIRA" they came to rely more on "WAUCONDA" or spring fields. The locations of "WAKU, WOC, WOK," (spring waters) were of primary importance then as the sources of clear well water are today. And to provide for his spiritual life, among many other things were his KIVA (Meditation Place) and MANITOU (Spirit of many talents, of a first order of magnitude).

What's In A Name?

Often the essence of a community can be captured in the names chosen for it. The sophisticated villages of "old New England" and the rough and tough pueblos of "the Far West" can generate an ambiance of personality beyond the mere words. City names developed such as PROVIDENCE, PHILADELPHIA, TOMBSTONE, WINDOW ROCK, PHOENIX and others.

But words and names change. Perhaps less now than before with our mass communications and electronic media. The history of place-names and words is a vast study in itself. Suffice to say that new words are being generated each year, and I am sure as many are probably dropping off into oblivion, suffering from lack of use or falling into distaste. Examples of new words generated in America in the last few decades are:

Word	Derivation	Orig. meaning
JEEP	Truck, G.P.	Army truck, general purpose
BLIMP	Balloon, limp	Army balloon, not rigid
MIGRAINE	Hemi-Cranium	Ocurring on one side of brain
BLIZZARD	BLZZ conditions	Weather code: blowing snow, zero ceiling, zero visibility
SMOG	Smoke/Fog	The combination
DUCK TAPE	Duct Tape	Heating Duct sealer
WOP	Without Papers	Immigrants not documented
COP	Chief of Police	Title
GRINGO	Green Coats	Yankee soldiers
YANKEE	Jahn Chee	Dutchman in America, or John Cheese (as English, John Bull)
AWFUL	AWE FULL	Full of respect, awe.
MODEM	Mod/Demod	Modulator/demodulator of data

How soon will our next generations lose the original derivation of these words, their reason-for-being finally lost to history?

The incorporation of new words and the appropriation of words from other languages into our American vocabulary is an ongoing function that can keep our dictionary-makers very busy. It is no wonder then that the early continent as large as North America would have many dialects and possibly even different basic language.

While we have little written records of prehistoric language in the Americas[2], we do have ample versions of their verbal language. Place names and sources of food appear on early maps as Indian names for which the meanings in many instances has been lost.

Many of these examples have been kept for us through the thoughtful foresight of our ancestors. Many also have been twisted by the tongue of the ethnic translator. It is surprising then, to see from this legacy the possiblity of a certain amount of uniformity, particularly in the basic needs of people: Food, water, and travel.

---

[1] *"Hiawatha" also a poem by Longfellow, reconstructed from Schoolcrofts notes.*

[2] *Many primitive American stone etchings are being studied, looking for ancient influence. The Epigraphic Society (headquartered in San Diego) has published several important studies.*

FIG 5.3

THE NIAGARA FALLS,
AS SEEN BY FR. HENNEPIN IN 1697.

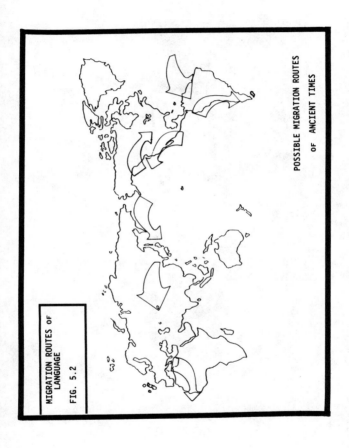

MIGRATION ROUTES OF
LANGUAGE

FIG. 5.2

POSSIBLE MIGRATION ROUTES
OF ANCIENT TIMES

SOME DAY

5. The Americas– Through the Looking Glass

Students of American history have been strongly influenced by the many accounts of American pioneers, namely the Pilgrims, the settlers, the macho Western outdoorsmen and even the native Indian mythology, most of it written from the European point of view. **I see a different America.** One that fits together much more simply than that presented until now. An AMERICA of natural wealth and prosperity and busy activities in harmony with these abundances from ocean shore to shore.

This is as though we were to take **a new look at America**, with a viewpoint from Asia. By looking at America (North, Meso and South) **without a looking glass — we see the same images but they are clearer, more focused, they are not reversed.** This, in reverse, was a technique used years ago for childrens stories by Lewis Carroll. While I believe **we have been looking at a severely distorted image of the Americas through a looking glass**, this new perspective will give us a much more focused view. It is quite appropriate, 500 years after Columbus, that we do so. We can not wait any longer.

I have used a model of the early American Indian language developed from historical translations which corroborate the initial model. It is somewhat speculative, I admit, to branch out into the diverse names that abound around us — especially so when the ancient speakers have died leaving us for the most part with only probability. Nevertheless, statistics and probability can be powerful tools. They are often used in science to **bring order and new understanding from apparent chaos.**

Many times the circumstances and locations of word useage lead to the potential meanings. But it is important to remember that word phrases were popularly picked up and in some cases relocated to areas that were not exactly their origin. **Early maps generated by explorers** seem to hold the most accurate information. But we do indeed hold a great debt of gratitude to most of our early historians for attempting to make accurate records from a verbal language which is most difficult to the European ear.

For there appears to have been much movement between these American and Asiatic landmasses, and in both directions based on language useage. **Was the latest movement a large migration out of Japan and into North America** with a fairly recent settlement in the Canadian and northern USA? Was it a natural movement based on a language similarity deposited in those islands thousands of years before as a primitive language? These proposals may produce arguments that will take years of study to become an organized model.

What we do know is that about 2000 years ago the spoken language of the Japanese islands (which I show was in an archaic form, quite similar to that of the North American Indian) was in dire need to progress to a written language. There was increased trade with neighboring China. They needed a written language and they had none. The natural thing to do was to borrow the pictographs of the Chinese with whom they were trading on a routine basis. These ideographs were applied to the vocabulary for the main words that their society used. But, because the Chinese was quite a different language, and the Japanese had other sounds and grammar, they had to develop another written language (Hiragana) to supplement the Ideographs (Kanji). This Hiragana was like an alphabet with about 46 phonetic symbols. This was during the HEINA Era. Later, as more European foreign words became popular an addition was even made to this phonetic alphabet which gave the Japanese the additional KATAKANA alphabet.

So, while the Japanese language when written looks similar to Chinese, it is not related to Chinese. Some studies link it more to Korean and I find it is directly related to the spoken language of the North American Indian. The native Americans may have taken the language to the islands originally. (Of course, the study of the other possibility — early Japanese developing the language and taking it to America could become popular except for some shortcomings)[1]. It is also apparent that the language used in common was also related to an early proto-language used by other ancient peoples of the world.

With this extraordinary viewpoint, let us take an imaginary trip through America, directly and not through the "Looking Glass" you might say. What do we find throughout the Americas? I believe we see a clearer picture of the culture, and a clear focus upon rich civilizations that both failed and flourished.

Our hypothetical traveler must cover such a large continent that at this time we will not concern ourselves with the tribal affiliations he would have to forge in order to easily accomplish his task of "tour guide of a new Continent". He will use the model of language developed, an archaic form of a modern language still in use today known as NIHONGO (Japanese language). Our time traveler is back 1000 years as he starts a fantastic voyage along Canadas eastern shore.

He is met with many lakes and wild animals to provide for him. Food, if you know where to look, is everywhere. The power of the Bow and Arrow allows him to be very successful against his prey, **and one very important advantage he has against larger animals is the technology of his arrowhead! It is the best available,** it is made of a special stone which also gives off fire, and called by the Indian, "KUWAI". It is the flint arrowhead, the Indians most important and cherished discovery! It could pierce the hide of the buffalo. In folklore, even Hiawatha stopped off on his trip to the DAKOTA country to trade for some of these arrowheads. As described in the next chapter, this famous place in Kansas was known throughout the Southwest as well.

The Blood Brother Clan
— The Ojibwa

There is a large brotherhood or clan in Canada with a common heritage of language and they are called the CHIPPEWA. Actually, this was the name Europeans gave them, while they more accurately called themselves OJIBWA. A young Scotsman (Grey Owl) who lived among them during the first part of our century reported the term to mean "Blood brothers". A more complete translation could be generated as "A blood relation society based on Uncle and Aunts" from OJI OB WA. This is exactly what the model from archaic Japanese produces. In fact, even until just a couple centuries ago, this is similar to the term the Samurai warriors of Japan used for themselves as a clan—they were the UJI (blood brothers) starting around 700 AD. Oddly, Japan appears to have been the last of modern nations to support a Warrior Class such as this. And even more coincidentally, **the SAMURAI were also known as "people of the Bow and Arrow"** as they courageously fought off the enemies whoever they might be.

A Nation Founded On the Power
of Algonquin

What a coincidence. The archaic translation of ALGONQUIN (ALI KAN KUWAI'n) also **means "TO BE OF THE BOW AND ARROW"**. While today YAJIRI and YUME are the accepted forms for arrowhead and bow we find **KUWAI as an old sound meaning "ARROWHEAD"** (now relegated to a botanical plant). **KAN appears in**

47

the language as a bough of wood held bent as a bow by leather sinews. It can be seen in such words as KANSHU (bow of a boat) and KANJIKI (a primitive snowshoe reported invented by Athabascan Indians) and even in CANOE. Such a proud proclamation by both the Native Indian and Japanese warrior classes reveals the strong nature of fraternal motivation that occurred in both. It is a trend that will be developed later in the identification of American tribal families and brotherhoods.

As in any large civilization, travel by river and lake kept the group within easy reach of fresh water and fish as well as making the transportation of heavy loads easy — for the wheel, while perhaps invented, appeared not to have been used. From neccesity, travel was a large part of the Native activities and without pack animals and smooth trails, travel by water was by far the easier. It is easy to understand the awe inspiring view as each new Indian generation on the Great Lakes waterways reached the giant water Falls at Ontario. Understandably, as the native reached these roaring cascades of water he called the region NIAGE RA **(NIAGARA) or "the Place of the DISCHARGE or EMPTYING"**. While today, BA (place) is recognized in Japan instead of RA, most of early America used the Indian sound "RA" (sometimes corrupted to LA). These great "NIAGE RA" Falls emptied the river waters into Lake Ontario in a display of overwhelming sound, power and omnipotence. Another ancient translation would be "Nothing but water makes a big sound — NYA GARA". This is also one of the several Indian pronunciations for this colorful area. The Niagara river empties into the Niagara Falls. The (lake) **entrance to the Niagara river was called "ERIE"** by the Indians, still today a popular Japanese word meaning "Entrance, or Inlet".[2]

Ontario — A Voice That Demands Humility

The south part of the Lake was known (in 1641) as ONTARIO to the Indians and much later, in 1867, the name was given to the entire Canadian province. The name ONTARIO is easily appreciated and understandable since **"ONTO RI YO" means "It has the rich, sonorous voice of the Gods, doesn't it?"** as it would be translated by model (Fig 5.3). It is no surprise then that reports from early Indians are that this is quite exactly what they reported it to mean **(It seems to be the voice of the Gods)**. For anyone hearing Niagara Falls and this modulated roar of intimidation for the first time, it is apparent that the awesome sound would evoke such humble thoughts. The low rumbling of the "voice" provided constant and subtle communication to the dwellers of the region—possibly giving rise to the popular **OTTAWA across the lake meaning "The SOUND" OTO WA**. However this seemed also to be reserved for any rapids or cataracts providing a sound along riverways everywhere from Canada to Kansas. The sound of these rapids is yet today a pleasant one to campers, knowing that the clear, aerated waters of the rapids can provide good drinking water.

A more sophisticated (possibly later) description for rivers having noisy, turbulent rapids is seen at Toronto. Here a shallow, noisy river was named MISSISSAUGA. Of course, the MISSI is water, or early name for a river and SAUGUA would identify it as **"noisy, turbulent river"**. This fast running river and rapids surely seems to fit this description. Today the word for "river" in Japan is "GAWA/KAWA". In India it is PA-NI, similar to the Phillipines. In both the Canadian Algonquin and California Callihua language, PA is the word for "river". Will the history of Japan show an ancient useage of PA for river; and can it provide for "dating" of language such as isotopes do for physical artifacts? Are there other indicators of words borrowed by the Japanese and native Americans from India and Tibet? Yes, and one seems to be "DALI, DALLAS, DELLES" meaning "steps, or stairway—possibly related also to DON, the steps up to a Temple". We see it used in the natural steps generated by erosion of river canyons, known in America as DELLS, and quite evident on the famous Wisconsin River.

Naming Of America, Country Of Rice

Passing through central Canada, Minnesota and Wisconsin would provide for rich supplies of wild rice as well as the huge numbers of migratory birds and fish all of which held more than just a passing interest in the minds of the semi-nomadic gourmets. For here in the thousands of potholes and rivers left by the ice-age glaciers grew vast amounts of rice which to this day is an important crop. In fact, WISCONSIN is reported to mean "RICE COUNTRY" in the language of the Chippewa. Actually, a translation using our model produces **"MAIN ROUTE of WILD COLD**

WEATHER RICE" for the various English and French versions of OUESCONSIN as being "WASE KANSIN". It might also appear in such places as WASECA (Minnesota) and WAUSAU (Wis) as well.

The famous Menominee Indians trace their name back to meaning "Rice people". The early name was MENOHMIN (MinneHoMI'nin) or "Water Grain" (rice) People". "The Place of Water Grain" was also an archaic name for the islands of Japan.

Other most important placenames surrounding shallow waters are **WINNEBAGO and OUENIPIGON** (original French for Winnipeg). While the G and K often have interchangeable sounds, the actual Menominee sound is reported to be **WINNEBEIKO. This, per the model, is "Superior rice crops" and is quite probably the same meaning for WINNIPEG.** By some Indian reports, WINNEBAGO means "People who dwell near dirty water". While indeed those Natives living near "WINNEBAGO" were often near the shallow, muddy waters that produced such excellent rice, I find it hard to believe that such an environment by itself would be attractive to these early settlers.

There was an abundance of wild rice throughout these regions of North America extending across the nation from Michigan to Oregon. The French recorded a lake NOQUBAY in Wisconsin, which if pronounced the same but spelled NOKO BEI would mean "DENSE RICE CROP". Why would there be such an extended interest in this delicious and nutritious food? Was

51

it a commodity not only well known all over ancient America but in Asia as well?

I believe so, for the Chinese pictogram characters that Japan uses for AMERICA mean "RICE COUNTRY". Now, to this day, it is most confusing to Japanese students who feel that America today is famous for anything but rice. (Fig. 15.1). **BEI KOKU means "RICE COUNTRY"** and would certainly be a fitting description based on migrating people leaving such an abundance of food to make the journey by either water or land across the inhospitable Bering straits. Interestingly, the Chinese used different symbols for AMERICA, putting together the pictographs that would indicate it was **BIKOKU "The country of BIG SHEEP"** (the complete Pictograph is popularly translated to "Beautiful country"). Could this mean the musk ox, the mammoth, or the bison? All have the same wooly appearance when grazing. It is a point for speculation and study— it seems more than mere coincidence.

Most of the early expeditions from Europe to these American continents were not made by people we could class as historians, scholars, humanitarians, or even explorers. Some might have been more aptly called "exploiters". Many left death and destruction in their trail and above all, many left misunderstanding. Even as late as 1803 much of North America had to be recorded during the Lewis and Clark expedition for the first time. The details of this travel were kept in a most organized manner as instructed by the U.S. Government. The point is, that much of what later observers saw as culture, language, and lifestyle had already been modified by 200 years of inter-action with the European contacts and culture.

Before the documented expeditions, **had the center of America been a rich organization, a far-flung EMPIRE having a basic language** in common? Could there have been a large empire of this magnitude without a common social or trade language? I do not believe so! There was a thriving empire — the Indians proclaimed it! And it has been RE-DISCOVERED in these chapters.

The first question often raised by people who understand the vast cultural empire of these con-tinents is, "Where did the people come from?" Were these native people primitive? Or were they modern people thrust into primitive surround-ings, cutoff from the cultural and trade centers they might have been earlier accustomed to. Many versions of these arguments can gain strength from a close study of the Americas, using this language model. We can not say the Indian was Japanese related for the reason that they both made use of a common language, any more than the Indians speaking Spanish in Mexico would be Spanish.

The language of the Americas is shown here to be widespread. How was it propagated? Two salient possibilities arise:

➤ It came over to America with a small group of natives having a common ancient language. They also went into the Japanese islands and a similar language was deposited there. This group of natives came either a southern route to middle or south America or they arrived by a northern route, the Aleutian/Bering theory. If they came by the south, could they have arrived from Africa/Arabia, across the Atlantic? Is the language of the Americas a direct relative of the Middle East, Hebrew/Arabic languages? If they came from the north, were they from the Euroasian plaines, related to the early Sumerians?

➤ The language was generated in the Americas and propagated to the Asia/Europe continents. It was one of two proto-languages to populate the globe. It would be spread by (barbaric) nomads across Asia and enter the middle East and become the ancient tongue of Mongols, Huns and Sumerians.

For decades scholars have sought in vain after the "Proto-language" of the world if one does exist. They have even sought after the **"AMERICAN PROTO-LANGUAGE"** that has seemed to exist, but escaped their detection. Wouldn't it be strange then if this American proto-language model were found to be related to an ancient world language?[3] I believe it is. Of course, some scholars have predicted that proto-languages will never be found! One of the leading experts in this field had no comment when advised by me of these amazing coincidences.

---

[1] *See chapter 14, The Second Discovery of America—and phrases used in Japan which appear to have originated in what is now the Midwest America, Mississippi valley society.*

[2] *The word IRI, EIRI, or URI means entrance, inlet, as we see here and in the word MISSOURI (Missu Uri). Actually the river entering the Mississippi at St. Louis was named by the Indians PAKITANOU (PA KITANOU) meaning "dirty river" based on its yellow sediment from the prairie lands. Early explorers heard the area where the river entered the Mississippi called MISSOURI but knew this name definitely did not mean "dirty river". So, for the last 450 years this has remained* **the mystery of the two names**! *PAKITANOU definitely (by this model) means "river that is not clean" (PA KITANAI). Of course, Missouri means literally " Water Inlet" to the Great River and described the immediate area around St. Louis, even the tribe encamped at that spot. Of interest to the KANGI reader of Japanese language, is the pictogram for this word. The symbol for "IRI" is almost identical to the Missouri geography of a river "inlet to a larger river". It's almost as though the Pictogram were "Made in America".*

[3] *Chapter 3 reveals a distant possibility of related Phoenician words to Japanese, such as word for SILK. However, both natives of Japan and America seem to use an even more ancient common language which in some ways appears related to early Sumerian or Scythian language and grammar. See Appendix A for writing similarities to Etruscan/Hungarian.*

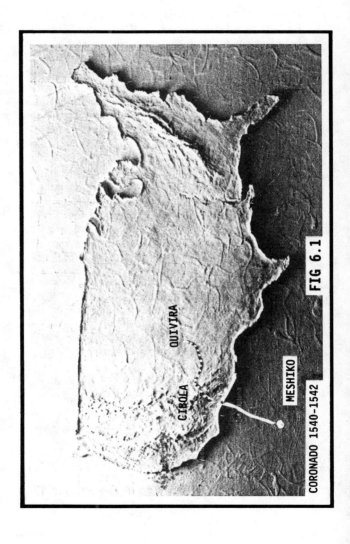

CORONADO 1540-1542

MESHIKO

CIBOLA

QUIVIRA

FIG 6.1

6. The Search For Quivira

America and Japan—Two Modern Countries Shaped By The Technology Of The Bow And Arrow

Just as the ship, airplane and the transistor have shaped the political, economic, and military futures of modern nations, so it appears that a seemingly insignificant invention of American peoples influenced empires. We have seen the early drawings of man attacking his adversaries, be they enemy or animal, with lances, clubs, and swords.

But judging from the linguistic evidence of both Japan and North America, **it was the bow and arrow that became the most powerful force** of conquest for them. Etchings from ancient American tombs reveal how important were the darts, dart-throwers and the Bow and Arrow to societies relying on them for political conquest. And the Samurai of feudal Japan claimed to be the UJI, blood brotherhood of the Bow and Arrow (UJI derived from simlar American OJIOBWA society).

Not only was it the arrow, fired with fearful accuracy long before the opponent could throw a dart or lance, but the significant improvement to the arrow by attaching the flint arrowhead to replace a simpler shaped stone. **The flint held two obvious advantages.**

First, the unique crystalline material could be chipped away leaving a narrow, razor sharp edge. Certainly, it's hardness like the glass obsidian made it easy to fracture as well, but the **profusion of this type of arrowhead (both intact and fractured) at Indian village sites is a silent testament to its acceptance by the serious hunter** (Fig. 3.2). And the knowledge of it seemed to have been known over most of the continent. The obsidian (glass-like, amorphous material) arrowheads seemed less precisely controllable and more fragile to make and use. And the simple stone arrowhead had been obsolete for centuries. Perhaps this flint arrowhead alone accounted for the dominance of the Indian over his prey animals and enemies.

The second advantage was psychological, for it was this same stone which provided them with fire sparks. To the spiritual mind of the Indian, could it have other mysterious intrinsic powers unexplained? Did this magical power instill in the natives a confidence and comradery that spread throughout the continent? Based on this language model, it at least held together the widespread family of the **ALGONQUIN — "To be the People of the Bow and flint Arrowhead". (ARU KAN KUWAI'n).**

The raw material from which to make arrowheads was evidently very important. Knowledge of it spread over most of America, judging by linguistic and archaelogical artifacts. It was also an important product of commerce.

My studies of Coronados search (in 1540) for the Golden Cities (CIBOLA) led me one day to

Kansas City. I had tracked by this language model, a mysterious object of his quest to the Kansas area and at this point I did not understand it. It was Quivira—! By my model language it did not mean "Golden Cities" but meant **"a place of Sparking Arrowhead" (KUWAI VI RA).**[1] Why should the Indian give this area such an important and strange name? What was a "SPARKING ARROWHEAD"? WHAT was so unusual about this strange place in the middle of Kansas?

Vern Cornett, an engineer who travels the area, soon answered my puzzling questions. This area, he explained, was one of the richest for finding this "Firestone" in the hills of Kansas, East of Wichita. This came as a pleasant surprise to me and certainly answered many of my questions.

Today there remains these rich reserves of flint which were located in the area the Indians called QUIVIRA. They are the Flint Hills of Kansas. The important location was shown on early maps and today many areas of Kansas as well as city streets as diverse as Overland Park and San Diego have this important Indian name.

It is the focus of a remarkable, yet pathetic story of Coronado and the Spanish Conquistadors. This happened almost 100 years before the English Puritan settlements of the Atlantic Coast. In some ways by using these new translations, it reads like a comic opera. For the first time in over 400 years, using the language, we can <u>now understand exactly what went wrong.</u>

The Trek By Spain Upon The Plain
Was Not In Vain

In the year 1541 Coronado in Mexico had heard of **the seven Gold cities of CIBOLA** but had not been successful in finding any clue to their whereabouts. He dispatched a large contingent of horses and people to find them, for by either fact or myth they were definitely located at CIBOLA. However, the real challenge came in knowing what CIBOLA was and how to get there. And here, after 500 years the language tells us Coronado made a big mistake. His failure was fore-ordained when he was directed to the wrong CIBOLA. Local opinion defined CIBOLA area to be some-where North[2] and old maps show it accurately (per the language model and Fig. 6.1). Reports vary, but some show that Captain Lopez de Cor-denas started out with as many as 300 men, 1000 horses, hundreds of sheep and 800 ser-vant/slaves. They left Mexico and headed into present-day Arizona (SONORA). While not im-mediately successful, one scouting group did manage to reach the Grand Canyon. Along the way they searched village by village with no leads but one. That came from one of his ser-vant/guides. He was an Indian nicknamed El Turco because of appearance and clothing.

He finally reported to the expedition an excit-ing revelation. He had learned from a village that **the wealth of the Empire could be found at QUIVIRA.** Some historians have surmised that this had been the original vicinity of his capture and he may have had a hidden desire to return to his people. This understanding, we shall see, will be clarified and El Turco vindicated at last.

The location of QUIVIRA was well known by the Indians. The large group marched off from Arizona with excitement at the prospect of reaching this important and legendary discovery. They changed course away from the Rocky Mountains off towards New Mexico and the Midwest. It seemed as though there may be vast golden cities which would even exceed the riches uncovered among Mayan and Aztec civilizatons. It might even rival the Peruvian plunder of Pizzaro in the Andes mountains, a few years before.

Along the way, there were native villages which encouraged them to move on. Historians surmised that the urging to move on may have come more from a desire to say farewell to this formidable force than to give them truthful advice. But, even if not what Coronodo wanted, it appears to have been accurate advice.

Based on our language model today, it is obvious that there was a gross misunderstanding between the Indian natives and Coronado. They did not understand what it was that could be found in the earth and was of such important interest to Coronado. They could think of only one thing, and they gave directions to Quivira. At least the direction was accurate. After many weeks of treacherous terrain **they arrived in what is now lower central KANSAS**, in the legendary region called by the Indians, **QUIVIRA!**

They crossed the Arkansas river into what was a pitiful village of permanent wood and grass huts built in a circle upon the empty hills and plain. It probably was what the French later identified as OUCHITA, or Wichita (houses in middle of a field— UCHI-TA). There were no golden cities, no "riches", only the forlorn families camped upon the apparently empty and desolate plain. We can imagine the bitter disappointment in the pitiful faces of these men—men who had travelled a thousand miles carrying strong steel armor and even stronger hopes and fantasies.

It seems that the Spaniards never thought to ask what such a desolate semi-permanent native encampment had found to use as a source for "trades-of-value". It didn't much matter anyway, for whatever the Indian had here, it certainly wasn't gold. And the Conquistadors were not interested.

Ironically, it now appears that Coronodos men had indeed found the secret wealth and power of the Indian nation but never understood it. For it lay before them everywhere upon the ground, revealed to the exploring party as an important mineral to be mined and exploited. The mineral was not gold, but flintstones! Had the Spanish been misunderstood or misled?

This was QUIVIRA, the "Place of the sparking Arrowhead stone". This was the place to which the Southwestern natives had directed the large Spanish expedition that was in search for an important mineral found in the earth. BUT IT WAS NOT GOLD. One can only imagine the intense disappointment. After dutifully (and erroneously it seems now) executing the guide who had "misled" them on a dreadful journey to this desolate encampment, the Conquistadors set out to return to Mexico.

They arrived in Mexico City in the fall of 1542 with only 100 followers. The rough terrain accounted for losing many men and much equipment, sheep and horses along the way. **And a most important fact**, the losses were not only to death but desertion and abandonment as well.

It's An Ill Wind That Blows No Good

Actually there were large benefits to both sides which came from this misguided and tragically comic tour of America's Southwest — the Spanish laid claim to large areas of the land based on this exploration. And the Indians gained access to stray sheep and horses[3], both of which they became adept at breeding. The Indian became an exceptionally skilled rider of the horses. This, it seems, gave the Western Indian a mobility and military posture that would later make him more difficult to conquer than any other previous Indians in the New World.

Many areas today exist in central Kansas where the hills are literally covered with Flint. The word QUIVIRA would be directly derived from the three words KUWAI, VI, and RA. Kuwai is the all pervasive word for Arrowhead while HI (modified to VI, just as in modern Nihongo) means "sun or spark". RA is "place". **Thus it is "The place of the sparking arrowhead stone".**

Today, most historians erroneously report Quivira to mean "The plains of Kansas" which indeed in a sense it would be, but that would not be the direct translation. Using our model of native American language, it could be explained exactly as above.

If Coronado Had The Foresight
Of Columbus

Had Coronodo outfitted his expedition with men that were familiar with archaic Japanese language, **the entire mission may have been scrubbed**, making the history of the Americas much different. Columbus, it is reported, on his initial voyage of discovery anticipated reaching the Chinese/India/Japanese coast by taking along with him an Arabic/Hebrew trader. This man would be able to act as translator for the expedition, and indeed, as you see in Chapter 3, this insight may have been more accurate than ever acknowledged or imagined until now. Coronado should have had this foresight.

For they would have known that QUIVIRA did not mean GOLDEN TREASURES, but was one of the most treasured symbols even beyond gold that the native had in technology. While GOLD to the Europeans had economic power and VALUE, the FLINT ARROWHEAD had real POWER! In hunting and in social conflict it had the Power respectively of both Life and Death.

And in Feudal Japan, the ancient Samurai also proclaimed themselves as a "society of the Blood Brothers "UJI—OJIOBWA", and also a society "of the Bow and Arrow." **The ancient name for Japan, YAMATO,** shows in its pictograph the man with the Arrow, "YA" hitting the "target— MATO".

Coronado would have also known that the mountain ranges down the continents of both South and North America could be called the "Backbone — CIBO" and a place to hide the golden cities that were sought. But it would appear that when he asked to go to CIBO-LA (Backbone/mountain place), he was sent to the wrong mountain ranges in North America. This range of mountains forming a cord or spine down the west side of two continents was even named by the Spanish, CORDILLERAS. When Coronado learned an important mineral was in the ground at the well-known place called QUIVIRA he assumed it was the gold he searched for. Had he instead gone south to the mountain places of Peru the gold would be easily found. But, alas, Pizzaro was already headed there and his dark deeds have been well recorded.

---

[1] *For clarification to the modern Japanese linguist, the term KUWAI is now relegated to the biological "Arrowhead" plant while the Arrow is YA. And HI is still used for "SUN, or SPARKING" which can be commonly modified to VI or BI to provide a more comfortable sound. RA of course, was dialectally changeable to LA or BA in the Americas, and today in Japan is "BA" meaning "the place".*

[2] *See also CIBOLA, chapt.7; note 3. CIBO was used to locate the mountain country of America and Cuba/Haiti. Primitive societies were early learners of anatomy. Through religious and funeral practices, the human body was the subject of much study. Through butchering for food all animals soon became objects of intense knowledge and of concern—perhaps mankinds first "scientific research" even before the flint spearhead. They were also quick to ascribe animal characteristics and features to the natural world around them. To some groups, the world was carried on the back of a turtle, and it appears here that Mother Earth had a backbone, and the mountain vertebrae were exposed to the world. Our language model reveals many rich metaphors throughout the Americas. CIBO LA would be a "place of Mountains" and held the golden cities, securely. INCA translates to both "Hiding place" and "Place of the People". Even Machu Picchu (Machi-Bi-Chu — "City belonging to the Heavenly Gods") was hidden far in the mountains. Was it one of the "Seven cities of Cibola"?*

[3] *The sheep lost on the expedition were from stock brought from Spain to Mexico in 1538 by Cortez. Among them were a hardy type called CHURRO. They adapted well and multiplied to millions. The wool produced was of a coarse texture, but highly suitable for the region and use in blankets. Through the centuries, an entire Navajo industry of herding and weaving was built upon these durable animals and their unique wool. Strangely, some of them had 4 horns   which occasionally is seen in descendants today.   courtesy Tanya Charter, and the Navajo-Churro Sheep Assoc. Ojo Cliente, N.M. 87549*

7. *The Weeping Earth Of Arizona*

How widespread was the language of the Americas? At first I thought the Canadian natives had a rather restricted range of language. It was quite surprising then to see that the language Model also fit Kansas (Wichita/Quivira Chap.6) and the great Southwest! According to the translations offered by HOPI and PAPAGO Indians of northern Mexico territory, they seemed to be using similar basic language as used by the OJIBWA indians around Wisconsin and Canada. Anthropology research tells us they spoke the Athabascan language. My thoughts are that **they are all closely related to a "proto-language"** which is here developed. By using this model, many Indian expressions become quite obvious and understandable for the first time.

The civilizations of meso-America (Mexico) are quite old, possibly older than those of North America. The center of Mexico territory, based on linguistics as well as early Spanish exploration, was located near the present day Mexico City and was called TENOCHTITLAN by the Aztec. And far north of Mexico City was the land of Sonora, near a desert-like land known for its abundance of hidden springs of water providing small but vital oases. You can spot them yet today by the tenacious growth of bushes and trees near them amidst the desert sand.

67

Today the landscape, based on Indian words, is quite different than what was seen long ago. Evidence of these water sources can be yet observed in a string of "wells and springs" across southern Arizona and California. The wells were certainly a welcome stopover for the European wagontrain traveler headed west and we can be sure they were not dug at random. Before the Colorado and Gila river were reduced by diversion, underground water pressure kept these springs running to provide for the people. The PAPAGO Indians reported that **the territory was described as such, "to be the area of small springs" — ALI SHO NAKU.**[1]

Except for the letter "N" this is the same name given the spring water area near Milwaukee, the area known as WAUKESHA (WAKU SHO), also having a rich source of springs. In contemporary language of Japanese this would be WAKU SHO meaning "Place where Spring originates from ground". But were the early explorers misunderstanding the word NAKU— should it have been WAKU ? No, it is probably just a matter of poetic expression on the part of the natural language of the Indian. For the word "NAKU" means "weeping" in modern Japanese and thus the translation for ARIZONA is more exactly **"To be the place (where the earth) weeps"**. A most perceptive way of describing these small but vital spots of desert "tears".

It is important to note that throughout America the natives used various forms of "TO BE", which were ALI, ARI, ARU of which the latter is now used in modern Japanese language. This was similar to the style reported by Prof. Jelinek of the

University of Sheffield for old style formal Japanese called BUNGO, used in government documents and poetry.[2] The addition of the "TO BE" to an adjective or noun is prevalent in this model of Indian language. ARIZONA then is reported to be derived from the Spanish dropping the consonant (K) ending and using ZO for the SHO of "originating place", that is, ARI SHO NA(KU) or ARI-ZO-NA.

The use of WAKU to denote a "spring" was not restricted to the Ojibwa of the northland—it was also used as far south as Florida. Here we see the popular springs near Tallahassee referred to as **WAKULLA, "the Spring place" (WAKU LA)**. This is a large natural spring which carries the Indian name WAKULLA and is obviously referring to the water coming from the earth, much as elsewhere in Florida. Throughout America we have towns and villages named SPRINGFIELD, which might have been called by the Indians "WAUCONDA" or WAKU'n DA, "a specific field of springs". The expression WAKU in modern Japanese has the same connotation, that of "water gushing from the ground"!

These sources of fresh water were often of life or death importance to these roaming people and we can see the respect, even the worship afforded these god-given events of nature. As in the village of Manitowoc, Wisconsin the Indian could imagine the benificent spirit Manitou which "rose up from the ground as does a Spring" (MANITOU WAKU) which local legend reports its meaning.

Before we leave the topic of FLORIDA, it is of interest to note one of the important and sentimental rivers leading across the state. It is the famous **SUWANNEE River, originating up near the Georgia swamp called OKEFENOKEE.** It is a swamp of immense proportions and colorful history. While the SUWANNEE River evokes thoughts of a romantic and beautiful past it comes somewhat as a shock to see that it translates simply **"From the Swamp or SAWA- NI.** Evidentally its name made famous by the Stephen Foster song identifies its origin as the dark, mysterious Georgia swamp.

As for ARIZONA, let us forget about some of the other proposed reasons for naming this state of Arizona. Some said it was from ARRID ZONE because of its desert conditions which today are fairly obvious. The derivation of the name as being from sources of water might surprise some, as it did me. While I might associate northern Arizona with rivers and water and snow, it certainly would not occur to me to see the association with the desolate southern part of todays Arizona.

Yet, as we look back at most of the Indian descriptions, they represent the **positive aspects of the land, the sources of food and water so necessary to their lifestyles.** And the land they knew may have been substantially more fertile, more watered than what we see today. We certainly must develop a strong respect for the early natives who without modern technology, worked and wandered throughout these "hostile" environments, met and employed (not conquered) nature on its own terms.

And in visiting the land of SONORA (That Garden Place) with its small springs scattered across the desert land, it is easy to understand why they called it ARIZONA—The place where the earth weeps. And in weeping, the earthly spirit MANITOU provided fresh spring water for his children – the American Indian!

But what an unexpected name the Mexican Indians called this area near Arizona north of Mexico City, **the SONORA! It seemed to me at first just a wasteland desert,** populated on the northern fringe by the Arizona small springs which in turn were guarded on the north by large forests of evergreen trees and mountain country. And the Gila river (Sunrise river) flowed into this desert. Based on the translation of SONORA, there must have been abundant water from the Gila and other mountain rivers which could be diverted to this area to support a rich agriculture. For Sonora would mean "GARDEN PLACE", a place where food cultivation (not just harvesting) was taking place.

Could there have been ancient canals dug here by the Indian civilization? Certainly the only way to support any type of "garden farming" in this area would be through irrigation. And if such was the case, then **most of northern Mexico knew and identified that this was "GARDEN COUNTRY" (Sono-ra).** Perhaps some day there will be found indications of large desert irrigation by non-nomadic people. With the greed of gold on their minds, it is clear to understand that the Spanish showed little interest in SONORA when CIBOLA (what was thought to mean The 7 golden cities) was their intention.[3]

71

Seeing that the language model works in Arizona (the model translation of "Arizona" is exactly what the Indians claimed), can it also help explain some of Californias place-names of Indian history? Not surprisingly it confirms the name the Indians gave the little town of **TEMECULA**, just north of San Diego, California. The description handed down by old natives of the original name TEMECURA is **"The place where the Sun peeks through (a fog)"**. Early morning fogs are quite common in this valley even today.

But that isn't quite what the Indians appeared to be saying! Again, in a poetic sort of way, TEMECURA (TE MAKU RA) can be readily translated using this language model to mean **"Place where Weather (or Heavens) form a Curtain (or tent)"**, TE (heavens) MAKU (tent) RA (place). Obviously, the word for "FOG or SUN" does not show up in the translation, but the primitive intent of the phrase amply describes it. And **from behind the Heavenly CURTAIN peeks the sun**. Anthropologists and professional linguists have claimed there is no language congruency between many Indian groups but for those "experts" looking for SUN or FOG in this translation, they will be disappointed and perhaps draw the wrong conclusion. One can see here that the literal translation has been lost to the native descendants, but the meaning survives.

But notice the immense problem for any American University scholar who sets out to translate such an expression from the Indian description! The expression "TEMECURA" has no word for "SUN" or "Peek" or "FOG" in it. Thus, all professors unfamiliar with Asiatic language, and having no Model such as I propose to guide them, **might never see the obvious (and primitively colorful)** correspondence. They might conclude that a different language is being used. As you can see, the primitive meanings are identical, although variously expressed. Here again I am led to believe that there was a dominant proto-language pervading all of the Americas.

A group of California Indians live in an area called CUYAMACA, which translates to (KU E AME KA), a "Place where the Rain comes from Heavens, KU-heavens E-goes/comes AME-rain KA-place" This is the ancient meaning of the area as reported by the Indians.

Many instances of "almost correct translation" also can be seen throughout America. The ANCIENT ONES, the ANASAZI, are a good example. The term "SAZI—SO JI" **means "Ancient people".** But it seems to have referred more specifically to those living in canyon caves or burrows since **"ANASAZI"** would have the literal translation of "ANCIENT **CAVE** PEOPLE".

The term for caves or burrows in the ground would be "ANA". It can be readily seen in Mexican and California areas called ANAHUAC. These are areas where water springs from small holes (burrows/caves) in the earth—ANA WAKU. Here, the Spanish influence of HUAC for the more English WAKU (semi-silent U) is obvious.

It extends even down to Peru, where the **Moche and Inca had HUACA (temples) of divine understanding (WAKA)** similar to the Sioux of the Midwest USA.[4]

You will notice in these chapters that we have crossed over the boundaries of states, and we have not divided the Indian nation into its usual tribal names and political entities. I see, of course, many dialects but not the vast unique languages so many·other researchers report. Of course, most of these scholars to whom I have talked have no knowledge of the Japanese language, a most powerful language spread over such vast continents! And related, it seems, to some of the earliest language of Euro-Asian civilization. Will it be possible, by using this model for language, to show that **there was a large ancient EMPIRE of related people here** in America, people willing and able to trade among these large areas for the common good? Will we see in a much larger sense a NATION where the knowledge and usefulness of QUIVIRA was only a small indicator of its farflung empire? An empire that not only "worshipped" the sparking arrowhead of Quivira but the SUN itself. I believe we are **looking back at a MISSISSIPPI valley civilization** that extended from coast to coast. Could such a widespread Empire of the Sun exist without some sort of common trade language? I think not.

Other Western Lands Of America

The Western lands of the United States are an amazing and overwhelming blend of grasslands, badlands, mountains, deserts and woodlands. Yet, in most all of these diverse environments, the Native Americans found a way to produce a living. **The descriptions of these lands by the Indians seems to accurately portray these states unique features** even if at times somewhat

74

misplaced. State names as recollected by natives and what that name would be determined from the language model are listed below:

Native name	Proposed by Indian history	DEFINED by MODEL
WYOMING	at the big flats	HOUSES HIGH UP
UTAH	high up	FLATS HIGH UP (MESA)
DAKOTA	friend, allies	STRANGE LAND
		FRIENDLY, FRAMEWORK, ALLIES
OREGON	river of the west	GEESE STOP-OVER PLACE
ARIZONA	place of small springs	PLACE OF SMALL SPRINGS

Many of today's landmark names do not seem to be exactly at the spot which the names describe. The territories were large and appeared to have had widespread recognition among the native Indians. But the popular names may have possibly come to rest upon specific areas just a bit removed from what they were meant for. With no need for a map, the traveler or nomadic hunter could easily remember the territories described thusly.

The **territory of UTAH "High fields or Mesas"** was a good description of these areas of Utah and Arizona. These large standing towers as well as the escarpments of fields which drop off precipitously into a deep canyon were surely no less a spectacular view 1500 years ago than they are today.

UTAH, denoted by Indians as a meaning which is quite in line with exactly what the model predicts—high UP—UE TA. This can be more accurately defined as fields or mesas which are elevated—the mesas at the top of the tall rock structures standing on the desert floor.

The territory of **"Houses high up"** as defined by WYOMING (UE NO MING) might more accurately define the Colorado area with its canyon walls supporting houses high above the floor below. Whether the people who lived in these houses were the ones to use the expression is left to conjecture. Or were they observed by marauding groups of other tribes—and if so, was this the basic reason the houses (villages) were built high into the canyon walls in the first place? It certainly appears to have been a defensive precaution, but highly vulnerable to seige.

MING was a word used for a permanent house as derived from an interesting village in northern Michigan, ISHPEMING. I determined a strong possibility that this would be close to the present-day but obsolete word, **ISHBEI MINKI (a house with stone walls)**. I asked a local historian what the village name, ISHPEMING meant. "We are not sure," was the answer, "but we think it means 'high up' because we overlook other areas." This sounded OK for WYOMING, but not too accurate for something as peculiar as stone walls, **so I boldly asked, "Where is the HOUSE with STONE WALLS?".**

"Oh", came the reply, "That is the famous old Burt House located several miles away, made with stones from the old quarry! It is an old landmark now used as a museum." The quarry had evidentally been a rich source of stone for many years and perhaps provided the Indian with early houses of stone. Or if it was of more recent origin, the erection of a house of stone must have been a strange and unique landmark to the Algonquin speaking Indians.

DAKOTA was reported by some Indians to mean "friend or ally" which by the model it can be translated. However, the similarity between the sounds might also make it "strange or badlands", a more probable explanation, I feel. Spelled also by the Sioux as LAKOTA, NAKOTA, this seems to be a well know area to the Indians who may have also included Kansas in the territory. For it was the Dakotas where legend put Hiawatha on his trip where he obtained arrowheads as well as the love of a young maiden.

Except for the nomadic hunting parties, could an Indian survive in this land? The sound DAKO can be translated both ways, "Badlands, or Friendly". Strangely, LAKOTA also meant a framework, like ribs on an animal, which individually and together holds the whole. **Rib Mountain** in Wisconsin had the **Indian name LAKOTA, and the name means "rib, or framework" in Japanese, as well.**

It would be a primitive but effective way to describe interactive support groups of "allies", so the collective framework was like ribs. Just as today, having Liver or Guts describes the courageous, so apparently the ribs described a framework of allies, like tentpoles in a wigwam.

The mystery of Oregon and its name remains. Some Indian reports show it as meaning "the River of the West"[5]; some report it as being named by a military fort commander who was transferred to the territory from Fort Mackinaw at upper Michigan. Both territories were on the flyway of millions of migratory waterfowl. **The midwest Mississippi flyway** had several places named by the Indians, Oregan/Horicon. They were stopover places for the migrating wild Geese. It is possible that the Oregon territory was known by the Indians for the flyway of the geese between northern Canada nesting grounds and the ancient wintering areas of California and Mexico. These would be **"stopover places, where geese come and go—ORAI GAN"**. These are today still important locations for the hunter of waterfowl (ie. the HORICON marsh area of central Wisconsin and Oregon along the Rock River of Illinois — both translate to GEESE COME AND GO). The huge migrations of geese yet persist in Oregon to this day. It is most probable then that the state name meant "GOOSE STOP-OVER" the same as the OREGON's of the midwest flyway. "Oregon" was important for it also meant fresh fowl for the campfire.

[1] *ALISHONAKU —The ending "U" is almost silent and imperceptible in verbal conversation. According to Hopi history, the Spanish dislike for an ending consonant caused the "k" to be dropped from ALISHONAK. Of course, ALI and ARI were pronounced in a similar manner, with ALI being replaced completely by ARI in Japan today.*

[2] *Classical Japanese-English Grammar Dictionary— (Jelinek; Univ. of Sheffield Press 1976.)*

[3] *CIBOLA was an important Spanish objective, and an accurate one too, if we use the language model. However, it does not mean gold, not even 'seven'. It would be "the place of the Backbone", similar to the mountains of Cuba/Haiti (Sebone). Indeed, Coronodo was directed up towards the American Rocky mountains, while I believe it was the Peruvian mountains that were the desired CIBOLA (SEBO LA). The Spaniards called the mountain string along the west coasts of the Americas "CORDIL-LERAS", meaning the Spine or Backbone, a direct translation of CIBOLA. It appears that it was popular to personify the mountains as the backbone of the earth. For there were no golden cities in the Rockies, but the "other place of the Mountains" contained many such cities filled with Inca gold and treasure which Pizzaro (not Coronado) would soon ravish.*

[4] *See also chapt. 16, Incas.*

[5] *The Cahuilla Indians of Southern California used "PA" to denote a river. (Cahuilla Dictionary, by Seiler & Hioki—Malki Musuem Press 1979). Midwest Indians also denoted river by "PA/MISSU /MINNE". Koreans use KANG, Chinese use HO, Phillipinos use BANE, and surprisingly in India the word is PANI. One of the major differences the Human race has over most animals is the rich and productive language use. The division and proliferation of human language is a most interesting study, but it is now time to bring the language barriers to an end. With worldwide electronic communication it is possible, and with political and social upheavals, it is imperative.*

8. Tribal Families Of The Americas

Evident in European family culture and particularly in that of semi-nomadic peoples, there is widespread use of relationships to identify people and their families. It is reported common from the Afghanistan nomads to the Brazilian jungle natives and is apparent as well in the North American Indian history. In fact, along with our language model it helps to explain, I feel, some of the apparent questions and mysteries reported by early explorers.

Let us look at the Kickapoo tribe, residing around the midwestern areas of Illinois and Wisconsin when first encountered. This was basically Ojibwa or Menominee area with the villages along Lake Michigan reported to be Potawatomi villages.

While the Kickapoo had much of the identical culture of these midwestern groups, early explorers reported that they seemed to have a much wider knowledge of the midwest American territory than their neighbors. A question arose as to why were they in this way different and how did it happen? **If their culture was so similar, why were they considered separate?**

If we use the model for translation of their family name we can arrive at a reasonable answer to both. Kickapoo would be derived from what is

today "kiku bu" meaning **"repatriated group"
returned to the family**. Had this faction of the
Ojibwa broken away and wandered through Illinois and the West, becoming intimately familiar
with the other great areas of America before
returning to again become a detached part of the
original family? It certainly would answer the
questions earlier raised. But, is this behavior common?

The answer is yes, if you look at the reported
lifestyles of the more primitive Yanomomo of
South America, factions of families can occur that
split off peacefully or otherwise.[1]

We might even see it linguistically in the
famous New York family of natives called the
Mohawk. They lived in close proximity to the
Algonquin group but were not always on the best
of terms. Some of this animosity may have been
used by the Europeans to recruit sympathizers to
one side or the other. At the battle of Champlain,
the Mohawks on the lakes east side were pit
against the Ojibwa on the west side. Yet, living so
close together for years before the European influx, how could this difference develop?

Here, again, their family name translates to the
"expelled" (HOKO) which implies that there was
a bigger, organized family from which they fled.
They may have gained a reputation as renegades.
Were they the "young Turks" of pre-Columbian
times? We can only use this proposed theory to
help us as a guide in our further understanding of
ancient behaviour and history.

Another group, the HURON was a family
around the Great Lakes. Were they just a nomadic

group of the other great tribes? It seems probable if we look at Huron as meaning "The Wanderers".

The cultural aspects of the tribal families as well as the way they dressed or ornamented themselves were key methods of retaining, recognizing, and respecting identities as the various tribal families wandered and interacted among other groups. As previously mentioned, it would seem that most all the Woodland culture of Indians could be related to the "ALGONQUIN Culture" as it is translated to "To be of the Bow and Arrowhead" (ARU KAN KUWAI'n). It was a widespread society based on the technology of flint arrowheads and special bows. The OJIBWA (Chippewa) were a social sub-group of this wide culture (OJIOBWA -"a Blood Brother society/ Uncle-Aunts"). By extension, we can also obtain:

IROQUOIS—to be of the Arrowhead

QUEBEC—another section of the Arrowhead

OSAGE—having hair braided down the bac"

APACHE COUNTRY —the magnificent, superior people or area

Of course, speculation certainly exists here for little accurate corroboration has been available.

Early maps of 1762 by the French showed the large area of the west to be dominated by the APPACHERIA. What kind of people would they be? Whether named by other tribes or self-named it seems a fitting name for such a dominant and colorful, active tribe. Maybe even egotistical. For, by use of the model, it would be **"place of people who are magnificent, exceptionally skilled"** (APPA-magnificent, CHI-people, RA-place). Certainly it could be an apt description for this dedicated group that managed an existence in such a hostile environment of desert and mountains. They would be known as **APACHES**.

These maps also show the land of the IL-LINOIS, another proud group who were met much earlier by DeSoto on his trip along the Mississippi. When asked to explain what Illinois meant, they reported **Illiniwek meant "magnificent men"**[2]. I am sure they had ample reasons to boast of this, as the Apaches did, but such large territories of the midwest were often more descriptive of the habitat, such as Michigan and Minnesota. Is this an instance where Appalachian people misunderstood the French questioners? Illinois would **translate to "Colorful Prairies"**.[3] These would be the prairielands of Illinois country, bright yellow or green with the seasons, perhaps swept clean of trees by regular fires raging across the flatland.

Is the use of NO for a prairie, a meadow, a grassland a common useage among the Algonquins? It seems it could be for even the state of NEW YORK was known as **GAN-NO NO** which would be **"GOOSE MEADOWS"**. New York, of course, was on the Atlantic flyway for geese and was a migration of immense proportions, dwindling to a trickle today.[4] Even parts of Canadian provinces and the Michigan territories were named (Michikamou—Flyway of Duck) after this most spectacular event. **The goose is a grazing bird, unlike the duck** which gets most of its sustenance from the water. The migrating geese need large amounts of energy which they get from grass meadows and fields of rice or grain. Thus, it is altogether fitting that the meadows of New York, maybe even the ancient shorelands across from Manhatten such as Bronx and Brooklyn were "goose meadows". At any rate, New York became known as the Empire State which sounds so much better than GANNONO.

The Mesquakie

This was a name used in Illiois to describe a group of Indians. One early account described them as having painted bodies, of a very unique color—neither red nor yellow but of some strange combination thereof. I should imagine this as a clay yellow or orange hue. But apparently the Natives had no such descriptive name, for in the model language this becomes "**Body of Red and Yellow" (ME SEQUAW KI)** (ME-body,SEKIWA-red,KI-yellow).

Some accounts of this coloring report that it was a method of protecting the body from insects and mosquitos. When first Atlantic coast settlers saw the Indian, they termed them RED MEN[5] now thought to be a wrong perception brought on by their skin coating, not the pigmentation coloring.

Notice that the color red was "SEQUAW" which is the same as used in the Indian word SEQUOIA (SEKI KUWA YA) meaning "RED ARROW HEAD". The absolutely straight shafts of red wood in these magnificent trees would make this an appropriate name. And "RED ARROW" was a popular name used throughout the northland, even becoming the designation for the famous Wisconsin Military division. A popular Indian chief took it for his name, Chief Sequoia. Red Arrows had special significance.

The **Navajos** also used such an expression (TSEGI) for a canyon of Arizona, famous for its overwhelming color of red earth (Canyon de Chelly). While current wisdom says that TSEGI means "canyon", it is felt that the sound is much like "SEKI" referring to the brilliant red canyon colors instead. The sounds are quite the same, and much different from any other such early expressions for "canyon". **It would appear to have been another example of misunderstanding that has helped perpetuate the myth that America was populated by people speaking 800 different languages!** I see a dominant archaic language closely related across the Americas.

Tribal Peoples Of Unique Culture

Where did our common names of North American Indian tribal families come from? Often the names today are what have been documented from the tribes first interfacing with the European. From this documenation, maps and reports were generated which helped to firm up those given names. And **many of these names were assigned by neigbors of the tribes,** describing attributes of identity to their appearance or culture.

In this way we see two of the great cultures of the southwest emerging as possibly something different than what history has recorded for us.

For the HOPI and YUMA Indian cultures (among others) have rather distinct practice. The Hopi culture includes the interaction of their spiritual beliefs with the activities of the snakes. Many groups, and indeed some modern religions, use the snake as part of their ceremonies. It was certainly a religious symbol of the Aztecs. The snake was quite active in the Hopi culture and some old maps show much of the area of the Southwest as being occupied by the SNAKE Indians. While reports indicated that interpreters felt that it was a derisive description made by the neighboring clans, it may have often only been a description of a peculiarity in their culture.[7]

Similarly, many cultures worship the interaction of their dreams with their lives. Some Japanese do today. Some of these cultures were in the Southwest and among three of them were the YUMA Indians. Special members of the tribe were selected, and after a few days away from home, they returned with accounts of their dreams to be interpreted as omens of fortune, good or bad.

Is it a coincidence then, that these names given these cultures do describe them exactly? For by using the model, HOPI means "snake" and YUMA means "dream"! Changes in pronunciation are outlined in the chart (Ch.12) for we are looking 1000 years or more into the past to reconstruct these words which today exist in more modern form in Asia. Some Anthropologists report that archaic languages more than 5000 years old can not be recovered. Languages that were verbal and had no written language are even more difficult to reconstruct. Sounds and emphasis change quickly under these conditions and only the most important words to a civilization seem to remain essentially intact.

At this point one might ask, can we use the model proposed for the (Canadian) Algonquin nation at these far-off locations of America's

Southwest? Is it still viable and how can we confirm it?

Yes, there is good affirmation that the Model is valid in this location, thousands of miles from the Canadian and Wisconsin territories from which the model was developed. As outlined in the previous chapter, the small Indian town in California about 40 miles north of the Mexican border is TEMECURA. The original name and that translated from the model matches. This, using the Model proposed, translates to **(TEN MAKU RA) "a place where the heavens (weather) forms a tent or curtain"**. The valley location is often filled with morning fog until the sun burns it away. So, surprisingly, the language used from Newfoundland to Mexico was similar.

The language model fits, making translations much the same as offered by the Indian legends. It also reveals some of the pitfalls which encumbered most early attempts at translation.

Many of the Indian translations were colorful, but not literal.

Waukesha, Home Of Football And Indian Legend

Today, Waukesha in Wisconsin is a city that relaxes in the distant glow of Milwaukee's industrial light. In recent past it was a center of heavy equipment and resort spas, it now serves as a growth area for westward expanding Milwaukee commerce.

Many of the modern streets follow the early roads which were developed to service the area including the old WATERTOWN PLANK ROAD, an early road made of wood planks wide enough to accomodate a wagon (but not to meet) between Watertown and Milwaukee. Occasionally wider areas allowed wagons and carriages to meet or pass.

These early roads were in turn used to replace old Indian trails leading to this most important area having utility both physical and spiritual. As in many parts of America, mounds of geometric or effigy design were found in abundance by the settlers.

But what was so important about this area? In its pristine purity with the (FOX) river located in a valley between rolling hills abounding with wild life and cultured corn it must have been a beautiful sight. The Indians used the hill of present Carroll College as a part of their village, and extending northward from there. The first white settlers in 1834 reported seeing possibly several hundred Potowatomie using the encampment of many wigwams.

Let us get our time perspective adjusted. Many of us, swept up in this century of immense technical progress, have forgotten how close we and our immediate ancestors are to the history of a fairly primitive lifestyle. Coal and oil provided most of our illumination and power. Many of our grandparents spent their youth travelling by horseback, buggy or sleigh. And except for the newly invented steam train, that was as fast as they could travel!

We can get help from sports fans in calibrating our perspective of TIME. Let's look at the record of football in Waukesha[6]. It was 1906, little more than 70 years after the founding of this little town in Wisconsin, which through its **football team gave us a new invention—the forward pass;** the first legal use.

St. Louis was the opposing team, hoping to play a weaker team, Carroll College. However, the college had been secretly practicing a new tactic just newly made legal, the forward pass. The sport of football had become dangerous and stagnant as brawny teams made frontal assaults on each other. The forward pass, at the insistence of Heisman, had just been made legal in 1905 and a way to use it had been devised by the college in the remote Wisconsin town of Waukesha.

The game in 1906 was tough, the half-time score 0-0. Then the secret practice sessions of Carrol College paid off. It was a surprising second half when St. Louis was overwhelmed by the new play! It ended 22-0 as the new play-plan decimated the competition. **The game, however, got little national attention** (as sporting games of Wisconsin understandably still often do today!) and it was not until 1913 that the play became famous when Notre Dame played Army. Knute Rockne used the pass play and brought it to national attention. And this was almost a century ago.

Has Waukesha become more famous for this than its Indian legend? Or have both legends been relegated to obscurity?

With that trivia digression, we can see that **we are still in a time frame very close, say 200 years, to the founding of this great country** as we see it today. We also must not lose the appreciation for the culture that the settlers found here. Why was Waukesha an important part of the Indian legend? **It was an area then, as it is today, of pure water springs arising from the ground.** These springs, aside from their value as sources of fresh, cold, clear water were also reputed to have rich therapeutic values as well. Using our language model, then, it is easy to see it as translated to WAKU SHO, "Place of Water Springs" (WAKU-Spring, SHO-beginning place).

With its location along the historical FOX river, it was close to water transportation not only to Lake Michigan, but to the rich wild rice areas inland that Wisconsin was famous for to the Indian. For Wisconsin meant "Rice country". These rice areas were along the Fox at WINNEBAGO (UE-NO-BEIKO) and the Wisconsin river (WASE-KANSEN). Here, **Winnebago translates to "Superior Rice harvest"** and **Wisconsin is "Main Rice Route"**.

With all this natural food of grain as well as an abundance of deer, this area had yet another advantage. It was on the natural flyway of the wild duck and goose that made twice annual stopovers on these lakes and marshes during migration. This area of America the Indian called **MICHI-GAN, and MICHI-KAMO—"the Flyway of the Goose and Duck"** (MICHI—flyway, pathway). It was not only a paradise for the fisher/hunter, it must have been what we can imagine as a gourmets delight as well. Tender goose on a pilaf of Wild Rice is a delicacy to be sought after and appreciated by outdoorsmen today. And it, of course, was all free for the effort.

Early settlers observed Indian corn being grown on the fields around Waukesha. This, when ground up into a powdery porridge, may have been called MAIZE just as the kernel corn came to be called. It seems a coincidence then that the grain ground into an edible powder was called MAIZE and the same sound, "MESHI, a ground up porridge" is used today in Japan being mainly rice.

At any rate, MAIZE was a well recognized food-plant throughout the Americas, having been cultivated for over a thousand years. In Japan, today, **MESHI means a "porridge (of ground up rice-grain)".** Rice is easier to grow in Japan than corn. At this point the intriguing **possibility arises that the language of Japan was "Made in America".** Or is it the reverse? Further insight of Chapter 14 can help answer this enigma.

---

[1] *See Chap 16, Yanomome*

[2] *The model develops "WEK" as a plural suffix such as used here and in the Menominee language. It is related to an ancient Eurasian langugae useage, that of the Huns.*

[3] *ILLONO— translating from French to Japanese ,IRO NO would be colored prairie. (IRO-colored, NO-prairies or grasslands). -wek is plural suffix.*

[4] *See Chap.10 on flyway statistics for Israel*

[5] *A popular name was SQUAM in New England, possibly meaning "RED BODY—SEKI WA ME" with a characteristic soft ending vowel. While ME is pertaining to the body, it is not a viable independent expression in Japan.*

[6] *From "Once Upon a Prairie" by Gil Koenig, retired editor; Waukesha Gazette*

[7] *The HOPI themselves ascribe their tribal identiy as "Peace".*

9. *The Spirit Of Manitou — A Guide For All Seasons*

A spirit of significant religious power extended over much of North America and guided the Indian, it seems, in a most natural and stimulating way. We have this heritage deeply inscribed upon this sacred land but I feel the millions of Americans who call this country "home" are scarcely aware of it.

Perhaps that is the way the ancient Indian would want it — for the **White man never understood this Indian spirit** which he might in some ways mistake for a god. It was MANITOU, and he was not a god but a subtle spirit which might be today equated in some small way to **"Mother earth"**. While there were gods that might look after the Indian tribal affairs such as the RAIN GOD, SUN GOD, etc. this unique spirit MANITOU permeated all of nature. He provided, sometimes in a whimsical manner, for his children, the Indians. He gave them all that they needed to pry out a comfortable existence from the wilderness as well as providing spiritual guidance of the highest level.

This spiritual guidance was from a source of "highest understanding" and "many talents" (MAN). This from the language model was

MANITOU (MAN ITTO). It would mean " MAN-wisdom or talents, ITTO-of the first magnitude". It was a spirit force having many talents and capabilities.

Manitou was particularly evident when his spirit dwelt beneath the ground, in fresh water springs, which he dispatched to the surface as cool, clear water in widely varying areas of the Americas. In many of these areas, it was a life-giving fountain of survival for the traveling Indian.

These vital springs dotted the landscape, often far away from the rivers that would ordinarily provide water and transportation for the tribal family. Not only were they in the hills of Canada and Americas northland, but they were discovered and welcomed by the Indians from Florida swamps to Arizona desert.

A place of spiritual and physical significance was the Indian "WAUCONDA", (WAKU'n-Spring, DA-field). Today, many states have cities named SPRINGFIELD and Illinois has a village named WAUCONDA as well as its capitol, SPRINGFIELD.[1] A campground near a field of fresh water springs, with animals and wild geese in abundance would be all that the Indian family could ask of the great provider, Manitou.

This great and many talented spirit seemed to have a particularly strong presence on islands. One can speculate whether this reflected a power within the microcosm of the island or perhaps a strong affinity of the Indians for some prehistoric island "home" from which Mexican legend proclaimed the group originated. Was it the legacy of AZTLAN?[2] Islands in the north of Lake Michigan were named both south and north MANITOU.

The village name of Manhattan is found many places in the midwest. The great island of New York harbor was named by the Dutch, **Manhattan.** Reportedly, it was sold by a tribe of Indians called the Manhattans. No doubt the name was derived with the Dutch accent from the Indian name for this sacred island, Manitou'n.[3] This story of the Dutch purchase must have been a gross misunderstanding. It is difficult to believe that a tribal family would name themselves after this capricious diety, and after naming the island after their MANITOU spirit, would then sell it to the Dutch. To paraphrase Shakespeare, "something smells in the state of New Amsterdam."

Does the spirit Manitou occasionally rise up, shaking the earth, reminding all its children, Indian and otherwise, not to despoil, but to respect its modern spirit position as "Mother Earth"? Today, happily, there are growing numbers of people intensely concerned with conservation and the environment, many even advocating a "back to nature" movement wherever possible. **It is perhaps these people who have also found "MANITOU" and understand him.**

The heavens have always been a source of mystery to primitive peoples and more directly, a source for religious interpretation and guidance. It was obvious that powerful forces flowed from the Sun, Moon, and stars. All records of early civilizations around the world are filled with the mythological explanations of the movements and birth of heavenly bodies. Reports of "medicine men" and priests providing a conduit to these potent forces are abundant in histories. Some are shamans claiming the creation of miracles and having animal spirit relationships. Some clarification of this ancient American structure based on language has been attempted to illuminate these holy forces in a slightly new perspective.

The elder or spirit leader of the clan was an intermediary between the tribe and the great god of the heavens which overlooked all things. This great god (of the Sioux) was WAKAN TENKA which no mere mortal could hope to emulate. The priest (medicine man) may be referred to as WAKAN, but **WAKAN TENKA** was reserved for the great master of the Universe. For this would mean **"Understanding of the Universe or Heavenly places"** which in the final analysis, no mortal Indian could hope to do. Astute and learned medicine men might gain immense training and knowledge becoming known and respected as WAKAN—a sort of priest who understands some of the heavens and spiritual workings.

For **WAKAN would mean "Understanding"** or **"Have Knowledge of"**. Today in Japan, to understand is "WAKA ARIMASU". Strangely, it was similarly used as names for priests or pyramid temples in the South American Inca Empire, thousands of miles away from the Sioux nation. While WAKA was reported to be a word derived from the Sioux language of the upper Mississippi valley, the reverse may be found to be more true— that the language of the North American Indians came up from Meso-America. More amazing observations on this topic will be developed later (Ch. 16).

The Wrong Manitou

An interesting sidelight to the spirits worshipped by the American natives is seen in the story of a great treaty meeting to be negotiated with the American government representatives. The night before, the chiefs and young braves attended a kick-off party which either by chance or malevolent foresight, had been heavily supplied with the demon liquor. The older chiefs felt understandably that it could impair the next days bargaining position or impair the ability of the young braves who were partaking in excess. They admonished the young ones, that they were now worshipping the **MACHI MANITOU** (MACHI GAI MANITOU) or **"wrong or mistaken Talented Spirits"**.

MACHII MANITOU	wrong Manitou Spirit
KITCHII MANITOU	lucky or good Manitou Spirit

In summary then, using the developed language model, MAN ITTO is still a viable but un-used translation today into "Wisdom or talents of the First Order or Magnitude". It was this spirit which we might call "Mother Earth" or "Nature", for in the Indian lore it was neither good nor evil, but looked after its Indian children with providence from the good earth. In some cases, it would spring from the ground, its embodiment being the spring-water such as the name "MANITOU-WAKU" (MANITOWOC, Wisconsin) which legend reports the city name to mean. In other places it dwelt on or under islands. Or maybe the glacier generated islands with their rocky backbone pushing up above the lake waters were the stony embodiment of this great spirit.

Clearly, this gave the Natives an important "Island Mentality" which is still operating and thriving among their modern cousins in today's Japan. Was it 2000 years ago that this culture based on the power of the Bow and Arrow reached (for the last and final time) the Japanese islands? Was it the Central American diefied SUN GOD that was installed in the islands by the colonizing forces from America? Forces that used the same self-description and title as later used by the SAMURAI ("OJIBWA" and "ALI KAN KUWAIN—blood brothers and people of the Bow and Arrow).[4] Was it the basis for the love of natural beauty in Japan, the development of the SHINTO religion and its spiritual ties to the natural world of animals? It seems probable that it is this ancient way of thinking, this tribal philosophy, this "KANGAIKATTE",[5] that drives the modern Economic Power of Japan! Chapter 18 treats this subject with more incisive detail.

---

[1] *It is difficult today to determine the useage in America of "popular Indian names" because as the postal service was expanded, many states having popular Indian village names had to remove the redundant ones.*

[2] *For derivation of AZTLAN, see Ch. 16.*

[3] *Here is the "n" adding specificity to a noun*

[4] ALGONQUIN—*Several American Indian names use both the ARI and ALI to express "to be" (see Arizona, Alaska). In Japan today, the "L" is non-existent, having been replaced by "R". In fact, it appears that one can go back in time and re-create the situations in America which produced some of todays Japanese words, ie: RACOON, KIGEN, KASHIKASKIA, BEIKOKU, KANSEZ, KAN-TOKEI. (see Ch.12 & 14)*

[5] *This "way of thinking", an attitude if you will, is perhaps a critical difference between modern Occidental and Oriental achievements. It is basic to tribal living.*

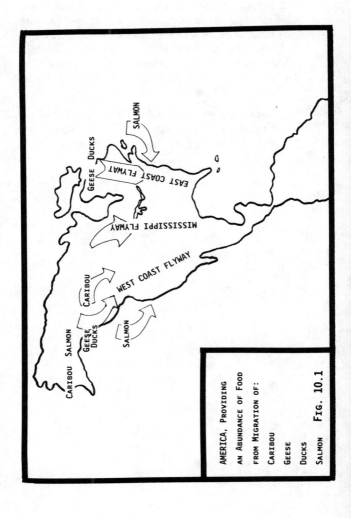

AMERICA, PROVIDING
AN ABUNDANCE OF FOOD
FROM MIGRATION OF:
CARIBOU
GEESE
DUCKS
SALMON

FIG. 10.1

10. Canada And Americas Great Northwest

The American midwest (North Central USA) and Wisconsin in particular has been acknow-ledged by some as the "Cultual Crossroads of Ancient America". It is described by the ancient Indians as a culture focused along and around the great Mississippi river which gave it access to a wide range of habitat. Michigan Territory had natural resources of copper and iron as well as lakes, wetlands, and moraines left by the receding glaciers of the last ice age. These along with the attendant fowl and animals provided all the necessities and many of the luxuries. Fresh water was abundant everywhere even away from the major water routes. Springs and spring fed lakes had been sprinkled generously among these states today known as Wisconsin, Minnesota, and Michigan. To a hunting/fishing society such as the "woodland Indian" the sources of ample prey animals and fresh water were paramount to exist-ence.

We can see this activity as the Mississippi valley culture. A rich heritage of language has been left to us by these important people of an American Lost Empire. A vocabulary of important phrases existed within the languages of the Indians when they met the early explorers and settlers. Perhaps the real meanings became gradually modified or misunderstood to leave us with a hodge-podge that shows little sensitivity to the needs that were so important. **Along the Great Lakes, using the language model, we can extract some interesting conclusions.**

Along the southern shores of the connecting straits between Lakes Superior and Huron is a very important territory known to the early explorers and map-makers as MICHI-LI-MACK-INAC. It spread across what is now the state of Michigan. An area popular with the French traders, it could be anglicized to the MAKINAW area with the center of the straits having an island called MAKINAW ISLAND. Certainly this was an important location to the native families living in and travelling throughout the area! But, why? Present day conventional language interpretation by the Indians leads one to assume it is a "land of the Turtle" for KANO is considered "turtle" in the local OJIBWA (actually, KANE is turtle in Japan). But this does not seem to do justice to such an important area name. Would the Indians in their wisdom, be that interested in turtles? No, it can use some further study to come up with a much more probable explanation and definition.

Looking further into the maps and stories of the explorers of these early times, some interesting analogies become obvious. First, we find the areas of Illinois, Wisconsin and Michigans upper peninsula with the name "MICHIGAMMEAU" and also "MICHIGAN". Obviously, there is an important "Pathway" here which is what MICHI means according to our model. In fact, you can even find along the shores of Newfoundland an area near

DUCK LAKE called "MICHIKAMOU". Allowing for French spelling and the popular trans-substitution of "K's and G's" we find this vital area has been identified by Indians with three different names:

MICHILI MAKAMO

MICHI KAMO

MICHI GAN

And how does a pathway through the Great Lake states and the Mississippi valley relate to a similar pathway along Americas East coast? Well, today, any young boy who pursues the outdoor life of hunting and fishing can immediately tell you that it is a "FLYWAY" that we are talking about, for migratory waterfowl! In fact, if we look at modern Japanese, all three of these describe migratory waterfowl; the first is "Flyway of the Mallard Duck" and the second is "Flyway of the Duck" and the last which in 1763 was finally decided as the official name for the state means "Flyway of the Goose". The "gan" sound derives from the exact sound the goose makes, which most naturalists will agree is more appropriate than "Honk". As for the MICHILI expression, even today a "long pathway" is expressed in early Japanese as CHILI as in CHILIYAMA, (Mountain pathway).

It seems that immense importance would be put on such a flyway where our early settlers remember times and areas when the sky was almost literally blackened by these migratory flights of magnificent birds. Even as I scanned the November skies years ago, they were often filled with the wedges and long stringy lines of honking geese on their long, lonely flight to southern wintering grounds. And for todays hunter, who under tight government regulations has managed to partake of these birds for his dinner table, it is an easy conclusion to see why the natives looked to these beautiful birds for sustenance.

And the spirit Manitou provided all this and much more for the Indian. For perspective, let us study some present-day migrations of birds. Because of their potentially dangerous migration route near Israel, migrating storks, eagles, warblers and other birds arriving over the middle East on their trips to Africa have been studied in detail. And today, amazing quantities of birds use this route because of its air thermals and location. Three routes from Europe and Russia converged into a corridor consisting of surprising quantities of birds along the eastern Mediterranean coast. A study showed 280 species of birds use this flyway, and an estimated total of 16 million birds on annual migration. This could be an immense hazard to air navigation today and is why the study was initiated. It gives us a perspective of what America bird migration must have been like a thousand years ago, before habitat predation by homo sapiens.

Back in the Americas, certain favorite landing spots for the birds seemed to be well marked by the Indians who, with the bow and arrow, could easily await them. Migrating birds must stop off to feed and replenish their energy. The place for "The coming and going of Geese" would be translated to "ORAIGAN, OREGAN, or Horicon" which we see alongside the Mississippi flyway as well as the West coast flyway. The famous Horicon marsh in Wisconsin, according to this name, had spent eternity playing host each year to geese that had made this a "stopover place" (Fig 10.1).

One of the most colorful and memorable places of Indian life and lore is around the headwaters of the great Mississippi river. Some of our popular knowledge is based on the work of Longfellow, his "Poem of Hiawatha". It portrayed an interesting perspective of Indian life, even though much of it was received by Longfellow as second-hand. With any civilization not having an extensive written language, mythology and folklore was relied upon to pass along the history and legend of their people. Also, it is observed that direct names are seldom used and instead, a personal or group relationship, one to the other, is often substituted. This can be seen in the rich legacy of names in the **Minnesota** territory which has a unique, almost sacred heritage because it is the **starting point of the great Mississippi**. A river of this magnitude was a landmark that could not be overlooked, and its birthplace was an object of reverence and mystery. For people living along the valley that it carved out of Americas midwest it was a dynamic entity, yet a barrier as we will see later(Chap.14).

It is difficult today for people to imagine the force and destruction of such a wild river before it was bridled by dams and levees such as it is in modern times. During springtime storms the raging river would be an intimidation to all that beheld it. A translation that seems appropriate is "A river wild and swift" (—MISSU-river, SEPPI-swift). We see only a glimpse of this ancient fury today when a dam breaks or ice creates the buil-

107

dup of a natural dam that spreads havoc and flooding.

Near the starting point of this great river in Minnesota are the falls at Ft. Snelling. They were known as **"MINNEHAHA"** and were described by Longfellow as "laughing waters". This is close to the model translation, but more exactly would be "Mother of Waters" or the starting source of the river. MINNE is still a current but little used word meaning "water". SOTO is a starting place so **MINNESOTO would be "Starting Place of the River"**. Coincidentally, it would be a "fountain-head" which today in Japan is called a "Min-nemoto" where "moto" is a more modern version of "Origin, starting place". And straddling the great river near Winona, Minnesota are two cities with the intriguing names "Minnesota City" and "Fountain City" which according to the language model are direct translations, each of the other!

The town of WINONA, made famous in the HIAWATHA poem is very interesting. You may recall that Winona was the mother of the young brave Hiawatha. He travelled to the "DAKOTAS" to buy arrowheads and along the way met the beautiful Indian maiden. His mother, Winona, was the eldest daughter of NOKOMIS and that is what the name was reported to mean by the Indians — **WINONA,"the eldest daughter"**. Now, that is exactly what the expression would be using archaic language now known as Japanese. More **specifically it is translated to "First born or superior female" (UE NO ONNA -See Fig.15.1)** but pronounced the same, and of course would also mean "eldest daughter". What a striking coincidence!

Relationships were important, and based on above, the **"eldest brother" is "UE NO OTOKO" or WINNETKA.** This is the name of a small village just north of Chicago. The grandmother of Hiawatha, **NOKOMIS,** would be "Many Waters", obviously an accurate assessment for Minnesota today.

In fact, the encampment on the shores of beautiful Gitchii Gumi may have shown some poetic liberties being taken in the poem. For this lake is generally identified as being Lake Superior, treacherous in bad weather and many ocean-going vessels have gone to the bottom there. **UMI is an "inland sea or ocean"** and Kitchii Umi would be "a dangerous inland sea" which is indeed a proper description. The Eskimos of the Arctic also used UMI to identify the "Ocean". Their boat shells (YAKAN) were called **UMIYAK meaning "ocean going boat".** (see Fig. 11.1)

The identification of the starting point of the Mississippi river was apparently of great interest to the early dwellers of the Mississippi valley. Their mythology embraced this site as the "Mother of Waters" and all along the rivers course we can see an ancient civilization of large extent. This will be shown in Chapter 14 and in Fig. 14.1.

Of keen interest to historians is the Missouri river for it reached far across the plains. It collected it's yellow, muddy waters and emptied them into the Mississippi near St. Louis which was a very important part of the Indian Empire. Early explorers heard mixed stories for the name of the great Missouri river and most said the name was PAKITANOU. Some reported it was a spiritual river and canoes passing its entry into the Mississippi often threw flower offerings into the confluence. Others said it meant "muddy river" and the area where it entered the Mississippi was called MISSOURI. The Indian encampment there was also named similarly. Most settlers admitted that MISSOURI definitely did NOT mean muddy. Surprisingly, all this makes sense when you look at the language model for both **MISSOURI and PAKITANOU**. Indeed, it is PAKITANOU which is clearly "Dirty or muddy River" and Missouri is simply "river Inlet". The term URI is an inlet or bay, both of which we find at the place where the waters of the Missouri mix with those of the Mississippi. Another river in northern Illinois is called PECATONICA and would be "Place where the River is Muddy" (PA KITANOU KA). PA is today a recognized Indian name for "river". And we also see "inlet, URI/IRI" as the inlet to Niagara Falls, the lake ERIE.

A colorful phrase which was popular among many places that the Indian travelled was POTAWATOMI, in fact many of the villages along the river inlets to Lake Michigan visited by Europeans were identified as "POTAWATOMI" villages. I believe if you define these villages with the language model you discover it is a highly desireable location, "PA OTTAWA TOMEI". This is a "River place with noisy water that is Crystal Clear" (PA,river — OTOWA, noisy rapids— TOMEI, crystal clear). Any village so located could be called by this description. And if you wanted fresh, aerated, and drinkable water this is the place on the river to locate a village. Were these descriptive village locations used as the way necessary education was easily passed down through the generations? Did it discourage the new generations from locating their encampment near quiet backwaters which could harbor dangerous disease while appearing placid?

Colorful parts of the East coast of America and Canada are evident in the language of the OJIB-WA, if the model is used. The eastern coast of both Canada and America was an important source of food long before the Pilgrims arrived. Much of the names retained for posterity were the "important ones" to the Indian, not like the European settlers whose ties to England or Amsterdam often influenced their naming of places in the New World in a similar manner, either after people or political powers of the Old World. But, while the coastline of Boston offered a convenient stepping stone to this new world for the Pilgrims, it must have also offered a magnificent source of fishing and hunting to the American natives hundreds of years before Columbus. We can see this if we are able to reconstruct an **important word, Massachusetts** for it would mean **"The Fish have a Season of Duty or Obligation"**, or a spawning season. This would define a season holding great importance. The many rivers entering the ocean were natural spawning places for the salmon or trout that used them in the spring or fall seasons.

Not only fish, but migrating waterfowl along the Atlantic coast were of acute interest (Fig 10.1). This season for geese flights did not go unnoticed. It would be **a season of NARAGANSETT**. The **"season when Geese followed and copied each other, forming lines"**[1]. And the marshes and meadows along the ocean were places for the geese to stopover, places of opportunity for the Indian to catch abundant food which during the season, was unlimited.

While one can be sure that netting, trapping and catching birds and fish by any manner was possible, can you imagine the intense interest in these marshes and rivers during the migrating and spawning seasons? At this time of the year everyone who lives near the great lakes or oceans knows that the spawning season brings hundreds of thousands of fish right up to the shoreline. After swarming around the river entrances for a few days they embark, when the weather is right, upon the final leg of their migration to their river spawning beds. Here they will lay their eggs in the most suitable and protected places depending on their species, and either return to the ocean or as in the case of some salmon, they will quickly deteriorate and die. What a "spectacle" this must have presented to the early native fishermen who after aggressively pursuing the fish for months in open water, they suddenly appear along the lakeshore and are all within easy spearing distance!

MASU KI GAN (MUSKEGAN) would mean literally "Fish come to the Lakeshore" and can be seen as a city along the shores of Lake Michigan. And across the lake, at another city, Racine in Wisconsin, was another popular river originally known as **MUSKELLUNGE** (later re-named Root after the French meaning of the Indian name RASEN). It, too, reflected the intense interest in returning fish seeking to spawn. It would be **"Fish come all at same time or with dedication"**. Today, it is also the name of a unique fighting fish native to Wisconsin and parts of central Canada, but it apparently does not have such a spawning run, and as such is a misnomer.

Would the natives of northern America be interested in such spawning events and does it show up elsewhere? Of course, it is even more specific in the rivers of Canada where one river is called COULLONGE (contraction of MASU KURU ONGE) and another in Quebec province had been given the name **TOMOGONOPS**. This is quite clearly "Upstream or Sexual excitement to Spawn" as seen in the modern "TOMAGO-spawn or lay eggs, NOBSU-upstream" of Japanese language. On such spawning occasions the tribal families might count on harvesting enough fish to last them several months.

And perhaps in a moment of levity, our native grandfathers referred to a northern Canada outpost as "NOBS-MING". While the white man has been advised that it euphemistically means "Entrance to the Wilderness" it may be no accident that it translates to "House of Sexual Excitement". Was it the last frontier for northbound hunting parties, a memorable entrance to the "wilderness", a last fling at the pleasures of civilization?

No wonder, then, that these places and their names have been passed down through generations. For the many of us who have appreciated the fine cuisine of trout and salmon, both cooked and smoked, we can attest to the exquisite taste and judgement of these American natives. And it was free. It was the **spirit of the earth, Manitou**, providing for the Indian with a munificence that

113

was appreciated, extolled and perpetuated in their mythology.

The spirit, according to my language study, was everywhere present and while neither an exclusively good or bad spirit, it looked after the Indian with the benevolence of the Mother Earth. It was not what we would think of as a god. In fact, the spirit or talent seemed to dwell in the natural objects around and most assuredly within the surface of the Earth itself. It seemed to particularly dwell on and around islands. It would often manifest itself as a pure, cold gusher of spring water coming out of the ground. For the travelling natives, these sources of water were more than a diety, they were a necessity. Places like **WAUKESHA** in Wisconsin are today noted for their "artesian springs" where the water pressure from the Lake Superior head had literally forced water to spring up from the ground. No wonder then, that **WAKU SHO means exactly that — a "Place where Water Springs or Gushes up from the ground".** It is just a few miles west of Milwaukee.

Just 50 miles north of Milwaukee is the important Potawatomie town of **MANITOWOC** where the natives also reported it to mean **"Where the spirit Manitou sprang from the ground".** The same WAKU as in Waukesha, spelled differently today, but pronounced similarly. This is exactly the same meaning that our model develops.

In Lake Michigan along the north shore of the state of Michigan are two islands, South and North Manitou attesting to the widespread belief in Manitou, the Spirit which could look after his children in a land that could appear to be openly hostile. In fact, small towns in Wisconsin, Kansas, and other places of the midwest are named **MAN-HATTAN**. The expression **MANITOO'n** with the "n" ending appears to have been (as it is today in Japan) a suffix expressing specificity. The Dutch arrivals on the island of Manitoo'n in New York harbor, using their Dutch accent, christened this important island forever in an unknowing tribute to the great Indian spirit Manitou. May this Indian spirit forever attend to and look after this island and its ethnically diverse population.

The Search For Alaska — The Bridge to Asia

A shoreline of stunning historical significance exists along the Bering Sea, along the Alaska coast and down into the rugged coastline of California. Here, food appeared to be plentiful for those hardy people equipped to harvest it. Animal migration patterns put a plentiful supply of migratory waterfowl along this "Pathway". And the **sea mammals such as seals and sea lions were plentiful.** During the breeding seasons they would become quite vulnerable to the native hunter with club or arrow.[2]

Was it this popular sought-after food supply that left its name on these shores? It appears there is little doubt that these animals left their mark in the minds and vocabulary of the people of this chilly land of abundance.

The old native name for ALASKA was reported to be ALI-YESH-KA. It easily translates using our "language model" to a very interesting

115

history. For the name certainly means "TO BE" some thing or place. It proclaims this northern shoreline "TO BE THE PLACE OF THE ASHI"— **ALI ASHI KA!** And this would be the same animal hunted by the ESKIMO according to the description given by the North American Indians. While the Eskimo called themselves, INNUIT (IN-UE, the People of the North), they were referred to by the Indians as **ESKIMO,** "Eaters of raw meat". But the model more specifically describes them, **"ASHI KIMO — the Liver of Ashi, some animal — probably a sea mammal"** (See more detail in LIFESTYLES). But, of course, the ASHI is an old name for the SEA LION. This mammal was abundant along these shores.

So then, **ALI ASHIKA** would be the place of that proliferate sea mammal, the Sea Lion. We can only imagine the vast herds of these animals along the coast of Alaska and Canada for the early hunters. Many of these hunters were known as the **ATHABASCA** group of Indians, speaking a language related to a large part of north America and in fact, possibly the whole continent. From the Sea Lion came vital provisions for this civilization. The intestines were used to make bow strings and of course the flesh was a welcome source of meat. The stomachs could be used for oil bottles much as the Greeks used goat stomachs. And the fur was ideal for robes or trade with inland people. But how did these hunters of sea lions get their name?

Strangely, their name seems also to bear witness to the importance of the Sea Lion in their lifestyle. Their name, ATHABASCA relates to the archaic language of North America as **"The SEARCH-ING PLACE for SEA LION"** — (ASSA BA

116

SHIKA). [Note that the early Indian language had the "TH" sound, transposed to "S" in Japan today]. These are the well know Indian tribe which Anthropologists have studied so closely over many years. Without written records, the people themselves could have lost this translation after many hundreds of years.

In fact, in 1926 a Chinese anthropologist studying among the Athabascan for his doctorate at Michigan wrote an interesting report on their language. While he reported that he found no Asian (Chinese or Tibetan) influence in their language, I noticed from his report that there seems to be a decided similarity to the Japanese language, a language in which he had reported fluency. They were even using BA-SAN (BETSUNE) for "grandmother" (currently OBA-SAN, in Japan). And a primitive form of HANASU for "He speak" (HANE).

A Lifestyle Link To Japan

Certainly, this is more than mere coincidence and worthy of further investigation for there is a very specific and peculiar similarity with the ancient islands of JAPAN!

The question arises, would it be possible for such a sea mammal called ASHI to be important enough to leave its name as a legacy to the great territory of ALASKA as well as a large group of native hunters whose name became popular enough to spread over vast areas of the Northwest territories?

The answer is that the Sea Lion has a very direct and important connection with the Japanese islands as well as with Alaska and the Canadian Athabascan people. **It was also used as an early name for JAPAN.**

The Land Of Ashihara-No-Kuni

The archaic name for the Japanese islands was: ASHIHARA-NO-KUNI which meant "The Country of the SEA LION".

The sea lion apparently got its name, ASHI, as a description of its legs (ASHI) as it tried to walk on land—a difficult task. However, it was a bit easier to do than for the legless mammals having flippers which dragged themselves on their bellies onto the beach. The hind flippers of the sea lion perform more like legs. It belongs to the family scientists named "OTARIA STELLERI", similar to the frisky Otter. HARA is "belly" so the ASHIHARA would be an animal with "legs on its belly".

And another name for Japan was ASHIHARA-NO-MIZUHO-NO-KUNI describing it as Sea Lions and Rice (Water-grain—mizu ho)[3].

But here was an entire country (Japan) using the same animal name as was used in ALASKA. In recent times (900 AD based on dialect useage) as this precious prey animal disappeared from Japan's shores it is easy to see how the new "searching place for SEA LION — ATHABASCA" got its name along with the people and the great territory of ALASKA.

118

One can also find a similarity in how the Menominee Indian tribe got their name, meaning "Rice people—people of the Water-grain (MinneHO Mi NIN)". This will be covered later.

The name of the Sea Lion has, based on this study, gone down in history as having more widespread popularity than even the name "GEORGE WASHINGTON". And deservedly, when you consider the numbers of ancient coastal hunters in both America and Japan that depended so heavily on it for sustenance and the artifacts of their livlihood. Without Washington, our nation may have been little changed, but without the Sea Lion and the hunters seeking it, it would have been an entirely different American civilization.

---

[1] *Surprisingly, this strange,unique yet accurate variety of definitions is in modern Japanese dictionaries.*

[2] *One version of early migration to the Americas from Asia proposes that it was not a land route but island-hopping that brought the immigrants. This language model theory supports it. This would provide more food for the travelers, per Prof. Wm. Laughlin of University of Connecticut (U.S. News & World Report-Apr.2,1990). The proposed migration was thought to be following the whales as food source, but this language description seems to mark the sea lion specifically as the much easier, safer prey. In fact, the Aztec natives reported they did come from an* **island nation far away, AZTLAN (ASHI LA'n).** *Remarkable details of this are covered in Chapter 16.*

[3] *Other translations also show ASHIHARA as "floodplains of pampa grass, rice, or weed"*

DEVELOPMENT of Early TRAVEL Methods, as proposed by LINGUISTIC STUDY.

EARLY HARVESTING FROM THE SEA USING A
"SKIN KETTLE" BY THE
DORSETT ESKIMOS.

YAK
SKINS STRETCHED ON A FRAME
OF WOOD ---"YAKAN" or Kettle

LARGE BOAT FOR USE ON AN OCEAN, CALLED UMIYAK

SKINS STRETCHED ON LONG FRAMEWORK OF WOOD
SPARS, USED TO TRAVEL FROM PLACE TO PLACE
(SHORT TRIPS) CALLED "KAYOU YAKAN" (A
Skin Kettle For Short Trips) A "KAYAK"

DUGOUT CANOE, (NO SKINS) USED BY THE MAYAN
INDIANS CALLED A "KAYOU KU"

A Japanese Kettle
TODAY, CALLED YAKAN
IS METAL, FOR BOILING.

FIG 11.1

11. The Language That Reveals A Lifestyle

Let's see, for a moment, what the language picked up by early American adventurers really meant. Did the local native people know the derivation of their phrases? In some cases, words passed down through many native generations may have been modified or misunderstood.

My boyhood friend gave graphic illustration of this. His father had described a horse to him as "black as pitch". Soon this phrase became "pitch black" which could be expected. But the connotation was picked up that the noun-become-adjective of "pitch" had a meaning of "totally, completely". He was soon describing the white horses as "pitch white"! Languages appear to have abundant examples such as this.

Let's look at some of the Indian phrases. They are interesting and to the American history buff they seem to resolve several questions, trivial and otherwise.

From Tomahawk To Transistor

If there is one artifact of the American natives beside the Bow and Arrow that was the focus of awe, interest and respect it was the Indian hatchet, axe, or "Tomahawk". While it was often thought of as a weapon, some research (and my translation) shows it to have begun as a tool of immense utility to the travelling Indian. It could be a weapon as well as an implement to dig out roots, break off saplings for traps, or drive stakes into the ground. It's general usefulness shows in the translation of the word **TOMOHAWK to "a Companion that I carry by my side"**. This was where the tool was carried and has a strange kinship to what became later in Japan a cultural symbol, the sword.

For judging by the language useage, this item of convenience was quite important. In carrying it with one, there was a differentiation of just "carrying it" as one would carry a load of wood, food, or other burden. This companion (TOMO) was **carried at the waist (HAKU)** just as later would be used by the Samurai for their swords. In Japan today, Swords carried at the waist are "HAKU" and a different expression is used for carrying things like burdens. HAKU is used for this ceremonial symbol of power and position.

So it would appear that the TOMOHAWK might have been also an item of ceremonial importance and utility in the New World. Perhaps long before its modern counterpart, the Sword, became a fixture to the UJI clan today known as the Samurai of Japan. And this tool certainly fulfilled its name being a constant carrying companion as a stone-age implement. For today, TOMO has little changed, still meaning a friend or companion in Japan.

It's A Small World After All

How several hundred years, maybe a thousand years, can change a verbal language is difficult to evaluate. Most old languages that are reconstructed are done so based on the writings left by the users. But in this case, very little evidence has yet been shown that there was a prevalance of written language in North America. However it might be possible to see useage similarities in important items to family lifestyle such as the babies. All cultures take special pride in these new members of the tribal family and they were often referred to as a "papoose" in early accounts.

Here, using the model language, and allowing for small dialect change, the modern pronounciation of "BAMBUTSU" is similar and means "a CREATION". As used for the early life of infants, it is a natural description for these new little arrivals into the Indian world. And it has the connotation of being a "gift from God" that I am sure was and is the understanding of most societies, even today. It shows the warm family ties and a similar lack of gender in the description.

In many ways, the word CREATION in this way shows a sense of spirit and respect that seems somehow lacking in the simple English word BABY or the Italian BAMBINO! If all babies brought into the world were viewed honestly as CREATIONS of some divine spirit or power we perhaps might have entirely new perspective.

The Lone Ranger Had Tonto, An Understanding Friend

In the early days of radio, a thrilling program was brought to America by the midwest radio station WXYZ in Detroit. It was in the depths of the Depression when entertainment was eagerly absorbed by the masses of underemployed. The latest invention, Radio, was spreading over the land to provide a quality of culture and education never before known — and until television, never equalled. No video tube was needed for most of the adventure programs presented by radio; the mind of the listener could construct a stage or landscape having a splendor unequalled by the television kinescope soon to follow.

The program which became a legend was that of the Texas Ranger and his faithful Indian friend, Tonto. He was called the LONE RANGER as he travelled on his great white horse, Silver. The masked man remained incognito as he spread law and justice around the West.

His faithful companion, Tonto, called him "KIMO SABE" with a great amount of respect. I inquired among the afficionados of this great show and came up with very little on the exact translation of what Tonto was really saying. Researchers said that the best they could determine was that it meant "faithful friend" or "trusty scout". Had the writers lost the original meaning? Both of these translations are a little bland for such a close relationship which the writers had developed for these characters.

It is not surprising to find when the language model is applied, as to what Tonto was calling the masked man. **For KIMO SABE would be an archaic form of "COURAGEOUS LONER"** or one who is a "GUTTSY SOLITARY PERSON"! There is no doubt that this is a **most accurate description of the Lone Ranger** and reflects the research the writers of the program put into it. Did they consult with a group of the midwest Indians to establish this name? Of course it seems quite probable and possible for the writers for the Detroit station to have researched this most descriptive OJIBWA name.

Today in Japan the ancient meaning of KIMO has been lost to the younger generation. They see it as meaning "Courageous" in its more current meaning rather than its derivation from the archaic "Liver" that appears in older documents. No doubt it came about much as the Europeans now refer to a courageous person as having "guts". It also would refer to having "Liver" as this was the organ of the body suspected since antiquity as being the source of courage and strength. While most societies do not refer to the liver directly anymore, it was obviously a source of speculation for good health, strength and courage. In fact, it leads us to another mis-interpretation of ethnic culture.

The Eskimo And His Indian Neighbors

The presence of the Indian over the entire North American continent is well documented and is a tribute to his ability to survive over a wide range of environment. Having spent most of my early years in the cold winters of Wisconsin, I soon learned a healthy respect for the Native Americans who had left evidence of their living in the thick woods behind our log cabin. Ceremonial (or burial) mounds were evident there along a small creek. The mounds had been grown over with tall trees and very little remained as physical features of these mounds that faced East/West. The early campground could be located as well by the large numbers of flint arrowheads and spear points that were lurking just under the ground. For the natives to survive these winters without modern enclosures or clothing must have been something just short of a miracle.

Yet, not only did the early Wisconsin natives live in this climate, they also ranged far up into the Canadian wilderness. At this point, they came into contact with the northern culture, the **people who they called ESKIMOS.** These people referred to themselves by other names (The Inuit — IN UE, people of the North using the model) but were called **ESKIMO by the Indians. This was translated by Indians to mean that they "ate raw meat".** This seemed to be a popular way to name various tribes encountered by referring to certain aspects of their culture or habits. In this case, using the model language, it is almost exactly what the Indian translation presents except it develops much more detail. It would translate to **"(Eaters) of Sea Lion liver".** Here is the KIMO which was earlier explained but in this case it is the liver of the sea lion which found such a fascination for the Indian. It was a habit of these Eskimo people to search and hunt for a seal or sea lion to kill. Upon the success of the hunt, it is still a common occurance for the hunter who has killed the seal to be awarded the fresh liver from the animal where it can be devoured at the site. This is the practice that has given to America the name for these hardy survivors of an impossible environment.

The Development Of Transportation

The Eskimos have an interesting relationship to the American Indians. They both relied heavily on water transportation and developed the versatile vehicles, the UMIYAK and KAYAK. The skins of animals (YAK) along with hot stones had been used for a long time to heat water for cooking. In some cases, these YAK skins were stretched over a sapling frame like an upside-down umbrella. They could be pushed along on top of the water, carrying food or people depending on size. Those big enough for ocean use were called UMIYAK.

Today, in Japan a YAKAN is a kettle for boiling water (now metal) and UMI is an "ocean".

The Indian natives of north America had large canoes but used a similar skin boat as the Eskimos did only made more long and slender. It was popularly used for short distances, for commuting from place to place. This verb (commuting) is KAYOU in Japanese which would make a KAYYAK a skin covered boat used for commuting, as opposed to the UMIYAK used on the ocean. See Fig. 11.1

The Perfect Circle — The Kiva

As in many cultures, the mystery and perfection of the circle was also evident to native Americans. Villages could be arranged in a circle with no one occupying a subsidiary position. And the four seasons always returned upon themselves completing the circle of life and death, summer and winter, migrating south and again north. All were cycles in the Indian life that revealed the

127

power of the circle, physically and spiritually. A circular place of meditation was built by the Southwest Indians. Here, in solitude or together, spiritual rebirth could be attained. These were referred to as **KIVA, and it seems more than a mere coincidence that this literally means "Meditation Place"** (KI VA).

Oddly, it seems that the Indian and Japanese both shared a rather unique ability to express profound thoughts and feelings in 1 or 2 syllable words. Unlike the Germanic and Dutch languages where complex expressions can be built from smaller words, this makes for some small words carrying many different, profound meanings. It can certainly complicate language reconstruction. And early explorers on the East coast reported they had noticed the Indian languages to have an abundance of the letter O and the sound W, both of which are characteristic of Japanese.

The House With Four Wives

In the early days of Kansas, there was reported[1] an Indian chief who was able to keep four wives. For this he evidentally became well known. He was adroit enough to keep them in four separate houses. He came to be called "(the Man) of Four Households" — CHITOPU. A city in Kansas perpetuates his paternal abilities with this name, FOUR HOUSEHOLDS (CHETOPU, KS). Not far west of there is another village, CHAUTAUQUA (SHI TAKU) which indeed does translate to "Four Households". Could this be just an early misunderstanding, or different pronunciations?

The Mexican Grasshopper And The American Buffalo

Such a dissimilar pair of lifeforms as the Grasshopper and the Buffalo form an interesting combination on the American continents. For the language model indicates that there was a thread of similarity in these two unlikely animals.

They both flew through the air!

In America the Indians had insects called PULGAS. It in some instances was the name for the common flea. At any rate, PUL seemed to be the name for a jumping insect. The Mexicans called the grasshopper a CHAPULIN (jumping insect) which also shows up as the Spanish word derived from the Americas. However, the basic grasshopper in Spanish was a SALTAMONTES (Salto meaning Jumping). In the New World, the Spanish soon learned the Indian word for **grasshopper, CHAPULTEPE.** It rolls off the tongue easily, and was also the Aztec name of a very important historical lake area near Mexico City — **CHAPULTEPEC, Grasshopper Lake.**

The grasshopper was an intriguing insect, **it could jump and at the same time make a flying leap through the air! It had wings.** In fact, using the language model, that is exactly what the word means:

> CHO—jumping
>
> PUL—insect
>
> TOBE—leaping, flying through the air
>
> KO—lake

which results in CHO PUL TOPE KO, the model language expression meaning **LAKE of the JUMPING INSECT that makes a FLYING LEAP**. So Chapultepec became known as "grasshopper lake".

While it is easy to see the grasshopper flying through the air it is much harder to visualize the American Bison, the Buffalo. Yet, in Kansas there is an area which is remembered for just that—**TOPEKA, Kansas.** For it translates to the **"Leaping through the Air Place"** or "Leap off a shelf".

TOBI—A flying Leap

KA—Place, location

For a thousand years this was a favorite way for the Indian to harvest the Buffalo. Remember, the pictures that you see of the Indian buffalo hunter astride his horse planting a lance or well placed arrow into these huge beasts is of recent history. Until the white man, there were no horses from which to attack this essential food source. And to hunt on foot was a most dangerous procedure.

The "Buffalo Jump" was an effective alternative as revealed in archaeological diggings in America and Canada. In the province of Alberta, I visited an area called "Head Smashed In" south of Calgary. The name amply and vividly **describes the method of dispatching the animals** after they had fallen to the bottom of the gorge and became disabled. How much more safer this was once the hunter was able to induce the stampeding buffalo to make the leap!

The historians have lost the original meaning for the area called TOPEKA (just as they have done for Kansez). But an ancient verbal language can be reconstructed with the help of modern computers and their ability to easily cross-link information. We are certainly now in the Information Age and can look back with an analytical eye to our colorful past. And it reveals the **unlikely similarity between the Bison and the Grasshopper.**

---

[1] *Indian Place Names (of Kansas), by Rydjord — D'Arcy McNickle Indian Library, Chicago.*

12. THE LANGUAGE of THE AMERICAS ©
THE INDIGO LANGUAGE
D. R. Smithana

A reconstruction of the Languages in America is proposed, called the INDIGO language. Some translations are verified by ancient records or speakers. (These are in BOLD). A column shows either ancient or modern NIHONGO (Language of Japan). This includes North, Meso, and South America. Because so few of our American ancient words are properly translated, some speculation is made where Verification is not available. The model develops as follows:

Words Relationally Organized
For Alphabetical, See Glossary This Chapter

(Indian) Indigo	(Japanese) Nihongo	English	Remarks
ALI	**ARU**		
ARI			
ARU	**ARU**	**to be**	L,R, often interchanged

133

(Indian) Indigo	(Japanese) Nihongo	English	Remarks
BA	BA	the place	
PA		river place	
RA		specific place	
LA		specific place	
KA		a Region place	
SHO,ZO	SHO,ZO	a (start) place	
UMI	UMI	Inland Sea	Eskimos use UMI for "ocean"
MINNE	MINNE	water/river	limited useage
MISSI	river		
MISSU	MIZU	water	
WINONA	UE NO ONNA	first born female	archaic
WINNETKA	UE NO OTOKO	first born male	
SHUU	SHUU	**bad or**	also SKUNK, peculiar smell as in Chicago
E'SHUU	E'SHUU	bad smell	also name for Chicago

(Indian) Indigo	(Japanese) Nihongo	English	Remarks
CHICAGO ESCHECAGOU	SHUU KA GO E'SHUU KA GO	**Village place** village of bad smell	Indian Skunk word same as "bad smell" in Japan
GO	GO	Village	
KO	KO	Lake	Maya, Aztec
NO	NO	Prairie, meadow	
NI	NI	from, in	
LI CHILI	LI,RI CHILI	long or a long route, geographical route	
MIAMI	ME a MI	navel	bud of fruit—center of activity
MENHOMIN MENOMINEE	**MINNE HO MI**'n MIN HO MI NIN	Water Grain people People of Rice	(RICE)

(Indian) Indigo	(Japanese) Nihongo	English	Remarks
KITANE	KITA-NI	in the North	
DAKOTA **LAKOTA** NAKOTA	DAKO **ROKKOTSU**	Friendly, Allies **RIB**, Framework	A supporting framework (Sioux)
ONTARIO	ONTO RI YO	**"Do you suppose it is the rich sonorous voice of the gods"** translation of Niagara noise	
NIAGE RA NYAGHE RA NYAGERA	NIAGE RA NYA GARA	Place of DISCHARGE Only water but makes big sound	The falls of Niagara alternate
WICHITA **OUCHITA**	**UCHITA** **UCHITA**	**Houses placed in a field** as at the Quivira mines in Kansas	
PA	GAWA/KAWA	river	

(Indian) Indigo	(Japanese) Nihongo	English	Remarks
OJIBWA, Chippewa	UJI or, OJI-OBWA	**a "group" of the clan, blood Uncle/Aunt soc** Samurai: were OJIOBWA called Blood brothers	
M'COSUN, MOCCASIN	M'KUTSU'n, ME KUTSU	**footwear** on body	early spelling now changedto Moccasin
ESKIMO	ASHI KIMO	Sea Lion Liver, (**raw meat eaters**)	Fresh Liveran Eskimodelicacy
INNUIT	IN UE	People of North	Northenmost
INCA	IN KA IN KA	Place of the people, secret place	alternate
CHI,JI,NIN,IN	JIN,NIN	People	used often
ALI YESH KA, ALASKA	ARU ASHI KA, ALI ASHI KA	"to be the place of Sea Lion"	Same name for ancient Japan
KIMO SABE	KIMO SABE	courageous "Loner" (gutsy, having liver) of Lone Ranger	

(Indian) Indigo	(Japanese) Nihongo	English	Remarks
ALGONQUIN, ALI KAN KUWAIN	ARU KAN KUWAI'n	to be of the Bow and Arrow	The Samurai called themselves "of the Bow & Arrow"
ALI SHO NAK,	ARU SHO NAKU	**to be the place** of little springs	Place of ARIZONA WEEPING EARTH
WAKAN TENKA	WAKARU TEN KA	**to understand the heavenly places**	this was the Supreme knowledge. Wakau was a priest (or in INCA useage was a temple)
MINNESOTA	MINNE SOTO, MINEMOTO	Water starting place, Fountainhead	
WISCONSIN, OUSECONSIN	WASE KANSIN	Main route for early rice Wild Rice	start of great Mississippi
MICHIGAN, MICHIGAMOU, MICHILIMACKINAC	MICHI GAN, MICHI KAMO, MICHI MAKAMO	Flyway (path) of wild GOOSE, Flyway of wild duck, Flyway of Mallard Duck	

(Indian) Indigo	(Japanese) Nihongo	English	Remarks
ALABAMA	ARU BAMIN	the Entire Nation	part of Empire
TENNESSEE	TENNO CHI	People of EMPIRE	also used to describe Mexico City, TENOCHTITLAN
TENOCHTITLAN	TENNO CHI HI LA'n	Place of the People of the RISING SUN EMPIRE	
KASKASKIA, KACHKACHIA	KASHI KOUKIA	Nobility people by Riverside	Capitol of Empire
CAHOKIA	KA HOKKEI	place abandoned	Abandoned mounds
SKOKIE	CHI KOUKI	Noble People	SHI KOKKEI
OGALLALA	OGARA RA	place of the tall structures	needle mesas, Rockies (L/R change)
OSAGE, OUSAGHE	OSA GE	having Hair braids down the back	

139

(Indian) Indigo	(Japanese) Nihongo	English	Remarks
YUMA	YUME	Dream culture	using dreams
HOPI	HEBI	Snake culture	using snakes
PAPOOSE	BAMBUTSU	a "creation"	a baby (P/B change)
KANSAS, KAN SEZ	KAN SAI	West of the "river barrier" (KAN), the Mississippi	
ARKANSAS	ARU KAN SAI	to be WEST of the "barrier" river	
KENTUCKY	KAN TO KEI KAN SAI KAN TO	Capitol City East West section East section	Capitol city (Kaskaskia area) Today it's the Osaka/Kyoto area Today it's the Tokyo area, east of "barrier"
WAUKESHA	WAKU SHO	Beginning place of Springs	Famous for water springs
MANITOWOC	Manito Waku	**Place where spirit Manito sprang from the earth like spring water**	**many springs**

(Indian) Indigo	(Japanese) Nihongo	English	Remarks
TOPEKA	TOBI KA	Place or shelf for Leaping or Jumping	Kansas Bison Jump
CHOPULTOPEC	**CHO PUL TOBI KO**	**Jumping Insect that Leaps and flies**	**Grasshopper Lake**
PULGAS	—	Flea, Insect	
KUWAI	KUWAI	Arrowhead	Old Japanese flower
QUIVIRA	KUWAI VI RA, KUWAI HI RA	Place of the "sun or sparking" arrowhead (Flint)	Kansas, New Mexico
MISSOURI, **PAKITANOU**	**MIZU URI,PA** KITANOU	**Water inlet bay, DIRTY RIVER**	**at St.Louis, both names used to describe entry into** Mississippi
ERIE	ERIE,IRI,URI	Inlet, entrance	To the Falls at Niagara
KALAMAZOO	KAGAMI MIZU, KAZE MIZU	**Looking Glass River,** Windy river	Both descriptions reported for this river.

141

(Indian) Indigo	(Japanese) Nihongo	English	Remarks
KAZE	KAZE	Windy	Kansez mistake
ISHPEMING	ISHBEI MINKI	House of Stone Walls	famous house in Michigan
TEMECULA, TEMECURA	TEN MAKU RA	**Weather(heavens)** form a curtain place	famous for Morning Fog
WINNIPEG OUINIPIGON WINNEBAGO WINNEBEIKO	UE NO BEIKO	Superior crops of wild rice	BEIKO is Menominee sound
POTAWATOMI	PA OTO WA TOMEI	River place where noisy water and water is crystal clear	Ideal spot for many villages
MASSACHUSETTS	MASU CHU SETTSU	Season of obligation for Fish spawning	
NARRAGANSET	NARA GAN SETTSU	Season for geese to form a line	migrating

(Indian) Indigo	(Japanese) Nihongo	English	Remarks
GANNONO	GAN NO NO	Goose Meadows	New York name
MUSKELLUNGE	MASU KURU ONGE/ONAJI	Fish come at the same time with duty	Return to river mouth to spawn
TAMAGONOPS	TOMAGO NOBUSU	Upstream to spawn with sexual excitement	Canadian river
TONOHPA	TONO PA	Bullfrog river	Calaveras, Ca.
MUSKEGON	MASU KI GAN	Fish come to shore	to spawn
WAUWATOSA	WAZ WATASO	to do a Portage	with canoe
QUEBEC	KUWAI BEKKO	Another group of the Arrowhead	Split off
IROQUOIS	ARU KUWAI	To be of the Arrowhead	

143

(Indian) Indigo	(Japanese) Nihongo	English	Remarks
SIOUX SOO	SOO SO	Pioneers, forefathers, Ancient ancestors	
ANASAZI	**ANA SO JI**	**Ancient Cave People**	Cave=ANA
CHOCKTAW	CHOCKTAI	Direct Descendants	
KICKAPOO	KIKI BU	Repatriated group	
MOHAWK	MO HOKO	Expelled, wander	
HURON	HURON	Wanderers, nomads	
APPARACHIA APACHE	APPA RA JI	People of excellent, fantastic place	Western America
GERONIMO JERENIMO	JI RONIN MO	Also a person of no master, no Lord. A Maverick	term for Samurai

(Indian) Indigo	(Japanese) Nihongo	English	Remarks
TOMAHAWK	TOMO HAKU	My companion carried from the waist	not carry in regular manner
OKEFENOKEE	OKI FUNA CHE	at intervals there is trembling earth	Peat hummocks in swamp are spongy
OKICHOBEE	OKI CHOBEI	at intervals, Last and Final	(fresh water?)
MANITOBA	MAN ITTO BA	Place of the Manitou	spirit
MANHATTAN	MANITOU'n	Spirit place (Dutch)	N.Y. Island
SAKAJIWAEA	SAGI JI WA	**Person of Crane spirit**	**Bird**
OSHKOSH OSHKOWESH	O'SHIKA WA CHI	Person of Deer spirit	
YANOMOME	**YA NO MOMO**	**Peach Fruit**	Tribal name

(Indian) Indigo	(Japanese) Nihongo	English	Remarks
KIVA	**KI BA**	**place of "Meditation mood"**	S.W. USA
MANITOU	MAN ITTO	Talents of the First order	spirit
CHILI	CHILI	long path, geographical	Chiriyama
CHILLICOTHE	CHILI KASSEI	Warpath, path of military assistance	route to War
CHILLIWAKI	CHILI WAKU	Path to hotsprings	Canada
CHIRICAHUA	CHILI KAWA	Path to River	Rio Grande
AZTLAN	**ASHI LA'n**	**Place (island) of** Sea Lion	Japan
ARIZONA ALISHONAK	**ARU SHO NAKU**	**To be place of small springs**	

(Indian) Indigo	(Japanese) Nihongo	English	Remarks
FUANA BAY FAUXE FOX	FUANA French English	Mistaken, false bay Green Bay	
WAMPUM	WAPPU	Allocation(money)	tokens
QUIPU	KIPPU	Allocation(tickets)	Inca system
MI	MI	Berry, fruit	vital food source
ELMIRA	ALI MI RA	To be place of fruits & nuts	popular place
ODEMIN, ODE	ODE	Heart or strawberry, greet with heart	open arms
TEOTIHOUCAN	**TEO CHI HOKAN**	**people are restored** their crowns in heaven	(Men can become gods in heaven)

147

(Indian) Indigo	(Japanese) Nihongo	English	Remarks
CUZCO, KU SHI KO	KU SHI KO	Universe starting place, **Navel of the Universe**	
MEXICO, ME SHI KO	ME SHI KO	**Bud start place (Navel) center**	
SONORA	SONO RA	Place of garden, planted food	Mexico area
MACHU PICCHU	MACHI BI CHU	Village possessed by Heavens	Andes
ANAHUAC	ANA WAKU	Ground springs, from burrow	cave
CUYAMACA	KU E AME KA	**Place Rain comes from Heavens**	
JACOPIN	WAKU BIN	People of Springs	Agua Caliente
JUACA, WAKA	WAKA	Temple, priest, "holy understanding"	

(Indian) Indigo	(Japanese) Nihongo	English	Remarks
HOUCAN	WAKAN	INCA temple, pyramid	Peru
HUARACHI	WARAJI	**sandal, footwear**	
BABOQUVIRI	BA BO QUIVIRA	Specific place for Flint	
TSEGI	SEKI	Red, not "canyon"	Canyon de Chelly
SEQUOIA	SEKI WA YA	Red Arrow, straight redwood tree	Red arrow
MAIZE	**MESHI**	**Ground up grain, porridge corn**	
ERIE URI,IRI	IRI,URI	Inlet, to Niagara falls	also inlet of MIZURI river
GOWANDA	GO WAN DA	Land of 5 bays (finger lakes)	N.Y.

(Indian) Indigo	(Japanese) Nihongo	English	Remarks
PLACOTA, LACOTA	**LOKOT'a,** ROKKOTSU	**Rib, framework,** to support and protect one another	ribs
ESCANABA	ASSA KANA BA	place to search for metal	copper, iron of Michigan
INNUIT	INN UE	Northernmost people	Eskimo

NOTE: Mayan language made up of sounds, 2 letter consonant-vowel,[1] C-V. The Japanese language is similar.

— WORD COINCIDENCE SUMMARY —

Observed above are cases of identical meanings (in bold print) between the American Indian language and words used in Japan. Those words that have probable same meanings show major correspondence and an interesting and close relationship.

GLOSSARY/Derivations ALPHBETICAL ©

(Some words appear only in older Japanese Dictionaries)

ALABAMA	from ALA BAMIN, ARU BAMIN; to be the entire Nation.
ALGONQUIN	from ALAKANKUWAI'n, ARU KAN KUWAI'n; to be of the Bow and Arrowhead.
APACHE	from APPARACHIA, APPA RA CHI; people of place of exceptional magnificence, Carolinas & Colorado areas.
APPALACHIA	from APPARACHIA, see APACHE
ALASKA	from ALI ESKA (ALEH ESHKA); to be place of the Sea Lion.
ALI/ARI/ARU	to be
ANAHUAC	from ANA WAKU, water springs from holes in ground, cave
ANASAZI	from ANA SO JI, Ancient cave people
ARIZONA	from ALI SHO NAku, ARU SHO WAKU; to be a place of Springs, or weeping earth.
ARKANSAS	from ARU KAN SAI; To be west of the Barrier (river)
ASHI	from ASHI (Legs), a Sea Lion, the current and old name
ASHI NO KUNI	Ancient name "Country of Sea Lion" for JAPAN
ASSA/ATHA	from ASSARU, search (for food)
ATHABASCA	from ASSA BA ASHIKA; hunting, searching place for Sea Lion (SHIKAG, elk, moose)
AZTEC	from ASHI TEK; "I AM FROM ASHI LA'n" (Japan); see TEK
AZTLAN	from ASHI LA'n, The Place of the Sea Lion.
CAHOKIA	from KA HOKKEI place abandoned.

151

CANADA	from KANA DA, land of Iron & Copper (metal)
CARI	from KARI, hunting
CARIB	from KARIBE; hunting ground or hunter (Cannibal)
CARIBBEAN	from CARIB; Hunting ground, specific.
CARIBOU	from CARIB BU; a group that "hunts" (for grass under the icy tundra)
CHAPULTEN	from CHO PUL, jumping insect, a flea.
CHAPULTOPEC	from CHO PUL TOBEI KO, Grasshopper Lake. From "Jumping insect that takes Flying Leap"
CHILLICOTHE	from MICHI-LI-KASSEI, (MI)CHI-LI-KASSEI; way of aggression or "War Path". (Chiliyama,mountainpath).
CHICAGO	from SHUU KA GO, ISHUU KA GO; Village place of Skunk or bad smell.
CHEATAQUA	spelled SHI TAKU, see CHITOPU
CHITOPU	from SHI TAKU; Four (4) households (in Kansas)
CHOCKTOW	from CHOKTAI ; the Direct descendents.
CREE	from CARI; Hunter
CUZCO	from KU SHI KO, place of Universe start, or navel
DAKOTA, LACOTA, NACOTA;	Allies, friends, "a framework that holds something together, a rib". from LOKKOTSU, a rib.
DENALI	from TEN ALI; to be of the Heavens. (Alaska Mt. McKinley). or DON ALI, to be the steps to Heaven.
ESCANABA	from ASSA KANA BA; place to search for metal.
ESKIMO	from ASHI KIMO; Sea Lion Livers (eaters of fresh livers of seals).
GAN	a Goose, from sound it makes

GANNONO — from GAN NO NO; fields of Geese, Goose meadows.
GILA — river; Sunrise river; from HI LA; place of the rising sun.
GOWANDA — from GO WAN DA; Five bays or\falls (Finger lakes, N.Y.).

HOPI — from HEPI, or HEBI; snake (or a clan that uses snakes as a large part of their culture).
HURON — to wander, roam
ILLINOIS — from IRO NOE, IRO NO; colored prairie or meadowland.
IROQUOIS — from ARU KUWA|; to be of the Arrowhead.
ISHPEMING — from ISHBEI MINK|; House having stone walls
JIRONIMO — from JI RONIN MO; also a person with no master, a maverick, an independent.

KANSAS — from KAN SEZ, KAN SAI; West of the Barrier (river)
KASKASKIA — from KASHI KOKKIA; Nobility place at riverside.
KENTUCKY — from KAN TO KEI; Capitol city East of the Barrier (Mississippi river barrier)
KITANE — from KITA NI; from or in the North
KICKAPOO — from KIKURU, KIKA BU; group repatriated or returned family to the tribe.
KIVA — from KI BA; Place of Meditation and deep thought.
MACHU PICCHU — from MACHI BI CHU; village possessed by the Heavens
MANHATTAN — from MANITO'n; (Dutch) MANITO'n place where resides the spirit of MANITO, often an Island.
MANITOBA — from MANITO BA; Place of the Manito spirit.
MANITOWOC — from MANITO WAKU; Spirit Manito springs up from the earth.
MASSACHUSETTS — from MASU CHU SETTSU; Trout (fish) have a Season of Duty or obligations (spawning).

MENOMINEE — from MINNE HO MI'n NIN: People of "water Grain" (Rice).

153

MESHIKO — from ME SHI KO, place of Bud start place; a navel
MICHIKAMAU — from MICHI KAMO, flyway of the Duck (Newfoundland)
MICHI-LI-MACKINAC — from MICHI-LI-MAKAMO (straits of Mackinac; flyway of the wild mallard duck.

MICHIGAN — from MICHIGAN; path or flyway of the wild Goose.
MINNESOTA — from MINNE SOTO (MINNEMOTO); the fountainhead (beginning of Mississippi river).

MINNETONKA — from MINNE OTOKO; Father or old man of Waters (Mississippi river or Missouri)
MINNEHAHA — from MINNE HAHA; Mother of Waters (Waterfall start of Mississippi at Ft. Snelling, Minnesota).

MISSISSIPPI — from MISSI SHIPPUI, MIZU SEPPU ; water (river) that is swift, wild and raging as the wind.
MISSISSAUGUA — from MISSI SAUGUA; water (river) that is turbulent and noisy, (shallow rapids)
MISSOURI — from MISSI URI; water (river) inlet (to the Mississippi)
MOCASSIN — from M'COSUN, M'KUTSU'n; body shoes, wear shoes.
MOHAWK — from MO HOKO ; expelled also
MUSKEGON — from MASU KI GAN; Trout come to the Shoreline (spawn)
MUSKELLUNGE — from MASU KURU ONAJI, MASU KURU ONGE; Trout (fish) that comes all at same time or with obligation (spawning).
NARAGANSETT — from NARA GAN SETTSU; Season when Geese form lines (flight migration).

NIAGARA — from NIAGE RA; place of the Discharge (of water).
NIAGARA — from NYA GARA; Only water but a Big Sound.
OGALLALA — from OGARA RA; place of Big structures, (Rockies—or large standing rock pillars)

OHIO — from O HI O; the glorified Rising Sun.

OJIBWA — (Chippewa) from OJI OBU WA; a clan or family of blood brothers. Uncle/Aunt society
OKIFENOKEE — from OKI FUNA CHE; at intervals, there is trembling earth. (Hummocks of peat marsh earth that are spongy, shaky and tremble when you walk on them).
OKICHOBEE — from OKI CHOBE!; at intervals, this is last and final (fresh water).
ONTARIO — from ONTO RI YO; it seems to be the rich, sonorous voice of the Gods. (Niagra falls sound)

ONTONAGAN — sound of the goose
OSAGE — from OUSAGHE, OSA GE; hair going (braided) down the back.
OSCEOLA — from ASSA O LA, Person of the Rising Sun
OTTAWA — from OTA WA; a noise, a river sound to be heard, a rapids.
PAKITANOU — from PA KITANAI; river that is muddy, dirty (original name for Missouri river)
PAPOOSE — from BAMBUTSU; a creation of God
PECATONICA — from PA KITA NAKA, river in the middle of North. (between Mississippi and Lake Michigan)
POTOWATOMI — from PA OTOWA TOMEI, where river has cataract sound and water is crystal clear.
QUEBEC — from KUWAI BEKKO; another group of the Arrowhead.
QUIVIRA — from KUWAI VI RA; place of the sparking Arrowhead (flint).
RACINE — from RA SEN; place along the route.
RAMONA — from RA MON; place of gateway (thru mountains).

SEMINOLE — a long outward journey.
SENECA — from SENEKA; riptide or water flows backwards (falls)

SHEBOYGAN	from UJI BU GAN, CHI BU GAN; Clan or relations along the lakeshore. (also CHEBOYGAN)
SHIAWASSEE	happy river, Michigan
SHOSHONI	from SHOSHO NI; from everywhere, near and far.
SKOKIE	from CHI KOKKIE People of Nobility
SOO or SIOUX	from SOO; pioneer ancestors
SUWANNEE (river)	from SAWA NI; from the swamp (Okefenokee).
TEK	suffix meaning " — I am from"
TEMECULA	from TEN MAKU RA, Place where weather or heavens form a curtain or tent (fog).
TENNESSEE	from TENN NO SEI; Heavenly life, Western empire, or also TENNO CHI; people of the empire.
TENOCHTITLAN	from TENNO CHI HI LA'n; the Place of the people of the Empire of the Rising Sun. (now Mexico City).
TEOTIHOUCAN	from TE O CHI HOUCAN, In HEAVEN People have their Crowns restored (Men can become gods in Heaven).
TOMAHAWK	from TOMO HAKU; a companion or "friend" that is carried below or at the belt.
TOMOGONOPS	(river in Canada) from TAMAGO NOBUSO; to be sexually excited and spawn upstream.
TOPEKA	from TOBI KA; Jumping or Leaping off Shelf or place.
UTAH	from U TAH, UE TA; mesas or fields high in the air.
WAKULLA	from WAKU LA, WAKU BA; place of the springs (Florida river)
WAUKESHA	Waku Sho; place of Springs
WAUWAUTOSA	from Waze Watasu Place of doing a Portage
WEK	suffix – indicating plural

WICHITA	from OUCHI TA, UCHI TA; houses in a field.
WINIPEG	from OUENOPIGON (French, see WINNEBAGO)
WINONA	from UE NO ONNA; first born female (eldest daughter)
WINNETKA	from UE NO OTOKO; first born male (eldest son)
WINNEBAGO	from UE NO BEIKO; superior rice crops
WINNEMUCCA	from UE NO MUGA; first born grandchild (eldest)
WINNECONNE	from UE NO KANAI; first wife, superior or top woman of polygomous household.
WISCONSIN	from OUISE KANSIN, WASE KANSIN; main route of Wild Rice

WYOMING	from UE NO MING, UE NO MINKI; houses high up (on canyon walls)
YUMA	from YUME; dreams (or a clan that uses dreams as a large part of their culture)
ZUNI	from ZUMI, a spring of water

Today, the **Japanese name for America is BEIKOKU, (Rice Country)** and we see solid evidence from language and artifacts that this was an **important crop of the northern America**. In fact, studies report that a cold weather rice was not indigent to Japan until late in their development. Was this brought over from the northern climates of Wisconsin and Canada? Rice with a short growing season (WASE) is known as early rice in Japan and WASE is a well used prefix throughout Minnesota and Wisconsin—Waseca, Wausau, Wausaukee.

The ancient name for Japan was ASHIHARA-NO-MIZUHO-NO-KUNI. This means it was the land of the Sea Lion and also "Water Grain" (MIZUHO—Rice).

It is interesting to note that **ALASKA** also translates "to be the place of the Sea Lion — ALI ASHI KA". And even more interesting is that a similar RICE name existed in the Americas as "WATER GRAIN—MINNE HO MI". This became the name of the Indian tribe in Wisconsin known as **"THE RICE PEOPLE"—MENHOME-NIN**, which became popularly called the MENOMINEE Indians.

We can not immediately **jump to conclusions as to ethnic relationships** merely because of linguistic similarities. No more than we can assume all people in New York City who speak English came from England. It is a starting place, however, for more detailed revelations which may have escaped previous scholars.

It may be quite easy to identify that the language of the Americas (native Indians) went to the Japanese islands several thousand years ago. And it also appears to have been imported back to America (in a more sophisticated form) in the last 1000 years. Not only can we learn from this language what the American Indians of both South and North America were describing, but we might **also gain new important insight into the Japanese culture and development which in many ways is an enigma to both Occidental and Oriental eyes.** Much work of brilliance has been accomplished by people showing the Chinese/Japanese influence on the cultures of middle America.[2] One of these books envisions trading trips here as early as 500 BC. — 2000 years BEFORE COLUMBUS. The culture similarity is outstanding and much beyond the probability of random coincidence.

Various scenarios may be presented as to how America and Japan shared such similar history. Two thousand years ago there was a documented influx of foreigners into Japan. About this time, a divine Emperor system was installed with Shinto religion having strong relationships to nature. A warrior society (later to become the Samurai) was formed called the UJI [OJIBWA (Uncle/Aunt blood brothers)]. The Indians were familiar with the Sea Lion as they hunted it up the coast of California and along the Alaskan islands. It was much safer and easier to prey upon than the mighty whales, and it provided them more of their necessities, including fur, oil, bowstrings, and storage (from stomachs) as well as the delicacy of liver for which the northern ASHI KIMO's (ESKIMOS) were famous.

Along the way, **perhaps even wild rice plants were introduced** into the northern Japanese islands. These plants would be a necessity in order to support large population densities. The **ground-up rice forms a rich porridge called MAIZE (MESHI)** not unlike that which was produced by corn all over the ancient Americas. Japan was much better suited to the raising of rice than corn.

Later migrations to the Japanese islands brought political methods even beyond the Emperor system which had reigned so admirably in Meso-America and possibly in the Mississippi valley as well. From America they exported the political philosophy of a divided continent— **divided into an EAST and WEST by a barrier;** A region east of the barrier having a capitol city called KENTUCKY (KAN TO KEI) and a region west of the barrier called KANSAS (KAN SEZ).

Of course there was no giant Mississippi river to divide the Japanese island of Honshu, so an **artificial line of demarcation was established** between the powerful cities of KYOTO and TOKYO. This **"barrier"** is effective to this day in separating the land into distinct and subtle cultural differences. The city of **Tokyo** (Eastern City) would become their modern KANTOKEI,[3] capitol city east of the Barrier. The East and West are also divided by modern electrical standards. In this century each separately contracted for American A.C. power generators—and one got 50 hertz, the other 60 hertz generators. The result is our common standard—50/60 hz alternating current appliances.

[1] *Scientific American, Aug. 1989 pg. 182*

[2] *NU SUN, by Gunnar Thompson published by Pioneer Publishing Co. Fresno, CA. 1989. It displays the startling design and culture similarity between Meso-America and that of the Oriental artifacts. With this language similarity to a modern Asiatic one, the groundwork is laid for more specific studies.*

[3] *KAN TO translates to East of barrier, while KEI is a capitol, lofty, high-up; a natural description of the ancient Mounds near KASKASKIA in Illinois.*

AMERICA, LAND OF THE RISING SUN

13. Japan — History Of Empire Of Japan

HISTORY of JAPANESE CULTURE

Short Notes on Historical PERIODS of Japan:

7000 or 8000 BC to about 200 or 300 BC
Jomon Period Noted For Coiled Rope Form Of Pottery.

4000 BC
Mongolian Influx, Generally Called "asians".

200/300 BC to 200/300 AD
Yayoi Period With Introduction Of New Pottery And Rice.

239 AD
Influx Of People From China, Korea

400 AD or before
Start Of Yamato Period, Influx Of Shinto Religion, And The (shaman) Queen, Himiko, To Start Shamanism. Start Of **Sun Line**, Emperor Related **To Sun God.**

500 AD approx—
Kanji Introduced To Japan From China. Ideograph Writing And Also Buddhism Brought By Korean And Chinese.

600 AD ASUKA period

700 AD NARA period

800 AD – 1200 HEIAN period
More Chinese & Korean Influence. Japanese
Alphabet

1200 -1300 KAMAKURA Period
Period Of Feudalism

1400 MUROMACHI Period

1500 America Discoverd By The Europeans.

1600 EDO period
Old Tokyo With Shoguns, Tokugawa Family To
Rule For 300 Years.

1853 Admiral Perry Visits Japan, To Open Trade

1868 MEIJI Restoration
To Modernize Japan And Enter The Competitive
World.

MODERN TIMES –
TAISHO regime
SHOWA regime to 1989 (Hirohito)
HEISEI regime starts in 1989 (present)

Various Theories of Ancient Civilizations

Summary of Japanese Theories
On Japanese Civilization

GEN NIHON SETSU — (original native theory)
Jomon people were "midgets" compared to
AINU, by Japanese anthropologist. This proposal
called KOROPOKKURU.

NIHON SETSU — points out there may have
been another unknown type of race of people
settling Japan islands.

NIHONJIN SETSU — (latest proposal) JOMON is the original people of Japan but there has been strong foreign influence.

The History Of Japan And European Influence

The trade routes from Europe to China were Big Business a thousand years ago. The SILK ROAD was what the caravan routes were called, reaching the rich trading areas of India and China.

It was the year 1271 when a group of traders went to China on a special mission that would mark it in history. Not so much on what it accomplished as for what its climax was. Three of the men on the journey were to become famous. **The young man Marco Polo, 18, was with his father and uncle,** who had just returned from a trip in 1269. Like many visitors to the Orient, they were dazzled by the ornate, rich, and colorful trappings of the kingdom as well as the large buildings and public works and bridges.

In their meeting with the Kublai Khan of Cathay (China) the Polos got along well and young Marco (now 21) became a favorite of the Khan. However, they were so helpful that they were denied leaving to return home. With various high-level assignments and travels for the Khan, Marco Polo would not return to his home in Venice for 24 years. It was this journey which was described so graphically in a book he wrote from prison (having been imprisoned by the neighboring Genoese state). It was hand copied in 1298 and became a famous revelation of a fabulous country and civilization. For the first time accurate common knowledge of the Orient started to spread among the Mediterranean merchants. Tales of the giant empire of China also included stories of the off-shore islands which Polo called CIPANGO, (Japan). Here, too, embellishment may have been added by the story-tellers as they reported golden bridges and rich silk cloths. But most of the views were accurate.

It was from accounts such as these that 200 years later, Columbus formulated his plans and aspirations of reaching by a Western route these rich lands to promote European trade. He first approached the Portugese Kingdom for they had been leaders in the maritime travels to explore the continent of Africa. With no firm committment from them (and possible double dealing), Columbus then tried the Spanish Crown and finally realized the success which has been quite widely documented.

The final chapter of the Western efforts to trade with the Orient was the trip by American Admiral Perry in 1853. The isolationism of these small islands would be breached but not demolished. The Empire of Japan would thrive and grow. So also would nationalism. Only history can now envisage the nucleus of roots from which its cultural growth and economic power would be derived. Who at the time could conjecture how deep these Japanese roots from ancient America had been? Who even suspected the roots were there?

14. Discovering The Hidden America — The Land Of The Rising Sun

At this point there is enough verification to start to suggest then, that the language model has some measure of validity, that the American Indian was using a language which we find today is in many ways related to a modern language. That language is NIHONGO, now refined and disciplined into a well structured Japanese language in Asia. (And that language in turn, may be related along with the Indian language to another ancient language spreading over four continents, but more on that later.) Not that our model is perfect but although missing parts, the parts that are there seem to form an extraordinarily good fit. With this as a base then, we might reconstruct, like the bones found by an archaelogist, the world that the Indian saw and talked about in ancient America.

It is as if we were to borrow a technique from Lewis Carroll in presenting what would seem to be a fantastic story — through a looking glass that reflects an entirely new view of Early America and it's inhabitants. A view of an early EMPIRE of the SUN, a rich Mississippi valley society which was powerful through technological advancement. This advance was the use of

the Fire Stone or flint arrowhead which made the Bow and Arrow a most formidable weapon.

The North American Continent which we often refer to as just "America" or "USA" is thought of often as having been a wilderness, a sparsely populated and unexplored no-mans land. A cursory examination of the records and activities of the new exploration parties to America can quickly dispel this foggy notion. Soon after Europeans hit the shores of North America (and South America, as well) there were maps generated showing details of these vast areas. Many details that could not have been generated by the explorers, but were gathered from the natives. The natives appeared to have as much or more knowledge of Americas geography than do many of our young students today.

The language and place-names left to us by these early inhabitants can only lead us to believe that there was a vast and mobile civilized society. We must call semi-nomadic people "civilized" even though Anthropologists may look for a written language and more urban villages to be more comfortable with the word. Except for Meso-America, few large archaelogical ruins have been left.

Digging in the ground reveals layer-by-layer the artifacts of great and ancient societies. So also, examining the languages left to us, reveals the thoughts and organization of an ancient people as we page layer-by-layer through their words expressing their ideas, observations and aspirations. All ancient civilizations used myth and mythology to substitute for the written communications we rely on today. Young people had passed down to them the history and understandings of their elders and forefathers. It is so much easier to understand and remember when history is in the form of song, poem, or mythical story.

It is startling to some scholars of culture to see how strikingly similar are the myths from widely diverse civilizations. Oceans apart, native societies cling to almost identical myths. It leads one (or at least those who subscribe to the diffusionist theory) to recognize that Man is the great Voyager, the great Technocrat. I believe the Human Race has been intelligent and nomadic over the last 5,000 years much more so than it has generally been given credit. When Man, a thousand years ago, left the Tribal Village, he lost a vital ingredient, collective wisdom.

We modern members of the "Information Age" have been given so much education, so much information and knowledge, that we tend to confuse it with "intelligence"! Knowledge we learn, intelligence we are born with. Wisdom (a form of judgement) and Intelligence have been Mans partner since he started walking on two legs. Man and his technology have experienced an almost exponential relationship with time. Through many products of technology, humans have been given whetstones upon which to sharpen their natural talent of intelligence.[3,4]

Digging Through Language For The Lost Empire Of America

By use of the language model to explore the United States a most amazing and compelling conclusion is reached. This was the beginning of a primitive EMPIRE, an EMPIRE OF THE SUN. It was closely related to the Meso-American SUN EMPIRES of the Aztec and Mayan and may have suffered a similar fate. At any rate, it appears to have been dead or dying by the time Europeans finally arrived to administer the final blow.

By studying the important Indian names left to us we can see the vast nature of this empire and understand the archaelogical findings which have mystified scholars for centuries. In America, particularly the Mid-west, many thousands of effigy mounds and mounds have been discovered. They are a link to the lost empire.

The central area of our country, TENNESSEE, leaps out of its quiet pastoral frame to take center stage in this new look of America—the American Empire. For it would translate roughly to the "Western Empire" (TENNO SAI).

If there were an empire of such widespread influence, there must be more indications. Of course, we know of the largest artifact of ancient civilization found in North America, the **famous MOUNDS along the Mississippi valley in Illinois** near St. Louis and Cahokia. Could this be part of the mystery? Historians report up to 40,000 people could have lived at this site and Kaskaskia[1] was still a large village area when Marquette passed through in the year 1673. In that village he estimated over 1500 people. It became the site for the first Illinois state capitol, as well. Today, a large museum has been built near there to focus understanding and education for this most important location and its ancient people.

Another beautiful area of America is what we now call ALABAMA. Here again political organization is seen in the territorial name which translates "to be the entire NATION". Was this just an egotistical term for a small group of underachievers. No, certainly not, for the language had spread also out into the Caribbean where it was first met by Columbus (Chap 3). The islands not far off shore are called by the natives, "BAMA" and the English spelling is BAHAMA. Did this also proclaim the farflung boundaries of a NATION that had expanded well into these island studded waters? Why did the natives of these islands, the Indians in Florida, and the Canadian and California Indians use a similar language to describe their environment? Is it a coincidence or was there a large nation, an EMPIRE of trade and social activity?

While most all early civilizations used Sun worship, we see here in the Americas (North, South and Meso) an intense and widespread useage of such worship. Woldwide, Kings and Emperors have claimed diety relationship with the celestial bodies and used this unique relation to give them a "right to rule". Until 1946 we even saw a modern version of this in Japan, perhaps one of the last great powers to change. The Emperor gave up his divine relationship (at the request of Army General MacArthur).

The similarity between the Japanese Empire and the EMPIRE of AMERICA is even more striking, and so amazing that at first might be termed unbelievable. The political structuring of early Japan is almost identical to the ancient political division in America as shown by the Indian language. This is not a trivial coincidence.

In America, the huge Mississippi River drains and divides a continent. It was an ambivalent friend to the native Americans who found it so useful for traffic and trade. For, in the springtime, swift and torrential waters moved down to the Gulf of Mexico unchecked by the modern dams. The river name translates to "SWIFT WATER" which during that time of the year is an understatement.[5] It could act as a "barrier" to the Empire, dividing it into the East and West, defining and seperating two large territories of ancient America: KANSAS and KENTUCKY. Among many translations of "KAN" is "barrier". And SEI/SAI is "west".

The early explorers along the Mississippi found and marked the area of the West side as the KAN SAI (French wrote it as Kansez, from which the English mis-understood to be Kansas) territory. From this developed the two states which today are known as KANSAS and ARKANSAS. They translate literally as follows:

KANSAS — West of the Barrier (river) Kan-sai

ARKANSAS — To be West of the Barrier Aru Kan-sai

Similarly, areas on the other side of the Mississippi became known as "East of the Barrier" where we see towns called CANTON (KAN TO'n) in Illinois and Ohio. But more importantly, we see the great state of KENTUCKY, being the area just adjacent to these great Mounds of antiquity located near KASKASKIA, Illinois. Kentucky not only translates as East of the Barrier, but as **"The**

Capitol City East of the Barrier"—KAN TO KEI. Could this have been the name for the Capitol of the Empire, the Empire of worship of the Rising Sun? Of course it was, if we listen to what the Indians were saying—it was KASKASKIA. This is "Place of the Nobility". Strangely, while it would translate to "Nobility by the Riverside" it also in Japan is an archaic word for **"Majestic" or "Emperor" but not a title**! Was this a word taken to Japan by the Native Americans during ancient migration to those islands?[1,3]

There can be little doubt that such an important part of the American Empire would have its reputation spread throughout the land. But might its presence also be hidden or denied to the European newcomers arriving yearly on Americas East coast? The explorers brought disease germs, the potential seeds of urban collapse. Perhaps epidemic was in some respect Natures way of explaining the mathematics of disease to these unfortunate souls.

For recent research shows that diseases that have incubation times are most destructive within statistically determined densities of population. Below this level, the disease microbe is unable to find a continuing suitable host. Above this density, an epidemic is probable if no other health efforts are used. Our modern health efforts continually elude the mathematical "odds" making large urban communities possible. Did the very size and nature of this capitol city which grew along the Mississippi river spell doom?

An Amazing Parallel

So, we have this vast Empire split in the middle by the great Mississippi river and with the Noble People living at the **Capitol City, KASKASKIA located near or on a giant Mound.** This capitol of the Empire is located just East of the River which marks the dividing line. The area is described as KANTOKEI (KAN TO KEI). Europeans called it KENTUCKY territory. Not far away is CAHOKIA, an abandoned location which has the interesting translation of "Place that was Abandoned —KA HOKEI".

But would an Empire allow itself to be "Split" by some barrier, and divide itself into a WEST (KANSAI) and an EAST (KANTO). Would it also refer to the area of its Capitol city as "KAN TO KEI" the Capitol City on the East side of the barrier?

KAN — A barrier, river

TO — East, eastern

KEI — a Capitol, lofty, high up

At this point, scholars of Japanese History and Language are probably sitting up in their chairs, shouting "BANZAI" or some other equally excited exclamation!

FOR THIS IS EXACTLY WHAT JAPAN HAS DONE!

They even use the **same names,** except the capitol city name is now Tokyo (East city). It is EAST of the Japanese "Barrier" just as "KAN-

TOKEI" is East of the Mississippi. It was not a capitol until later, when the capitol was relocated from Kyoto to EDO, the old name for Tokyo. Japan had no river barrier to naturally divide the islands so an artificial one had to be created. **Thus, today Japanese Honshu Island is divided into the Eastern and Western** cultural units by way of an approximate line just east of OSAKA. It is an **artificial Barrier** which divides Japan into KANSAI (west) and KANTO (east) sections that today have their own special dialects and mannerisms. Which way did this culture travel in its adoption? Was this manner of **political division brought to Japan at the same time that the SUN GOD** was installed (Himiko, about 2000 yrs ago)?[2,3]

The professional anthropologists have been pursuing their studies as a science for little more than 100 years. Often it seems they have limited interest in the heritage of language left to us. But I see a most interesting side of human evolution in language and logic. The human use of language accelerated evolution[6]. While artifacts tell us what their hands were doing, language tells us what their minds were thinking. It seems to identify the social aspects of technology, of mans civilized beginning, **and how primitive language evolves** in societies.

With further verification and development, these two continents and languages become a fantastic workshop for those interested in how language develops. For we have effectively a "motion picture show" of language development over the last 3000 years. We can study it, between America and Japan as in slow motion, the old and the new, a frame at a time.

1 *Early explorers stayed at this large village of KASKASKIA and reported 130 houses and approximately 2000 people living there. They also show it as spelled "KACH-KACHIA" which is a sound more in line with the modern Japanese word for EMPEROR (Kashikoki). Oddly, this word sound (not the Chinese characters) could be split to KASHI KOKI—"river-bank Nobility". And SHI KOKI (SKOKIE, SHKOKIE) would be "Noble people", a popular Indian campground near WINNETKA (elder brother), north of Chicago.*

2 *HIMIKO was reported to be the start of the SUN GOD line of Japan from which the ruling class was descended (until 1946 when MacArthur asked that divinity be denied). Work done by Anthropologist C.Loring Brace indicates that ancient skull structue of the ruling class of Japan (and Samurai) appear to be different from the Japanese multitudes. This might be explained by this study of language similarity from America. There are two simple schools of thought on the population of Japan by foreign intruders, they came from the South, or North. Certainly these primitive studies might help tip the scales.*

3 *If these words descriptive of Japanese royalty are accurate, then EMPEROR (KASHIKOKI) means "Nobility by Riverside" based on the Mississippi River passing near the capitol city East of the river barrier, KENTUCKY (KAN TOKEI). The direction of cultural travel during this time period then from America to the Japanese islands would seem to be quite definite.*

[4] *The amateur philosopher might muse over the proposal that technological advances are accelerated in a civilization that is predominantly maritime. Building a house that collapses is a problem, but building a boat that sinks becomes a tragedy. Thus ocean-going societies might be inclined to use their intelligence more expertly. They progress more rapidly toward what we consider modern living and artifacts. While civilization may not have started in the Mediterranean area, it was an ideal place to experiment and grow. However, the Pacific also seemed to be the dream and domain of ancient mariners. Interested readers are referred to the book "NU SUN" by Gunnar Thompson for a marine Asia-America connection.(Chap. 12, Note 1)*

[5] *Interestingly, today the ritual of SEPPEKU, Hari Kari by disembowlment is related to a "swift, pressure".*

[6] *The rapid increase in cultural growth among the human population over the past 20,000 years can perhaps be directly linked to communication, the use of Language. We see here, like all primitive languages, the simple generation of words for basic needs. Often (as in the Italian language, MANGIARI-MANO) the word for "eat" can have the expression for "hand" or "mid-section of body" as part of it.*

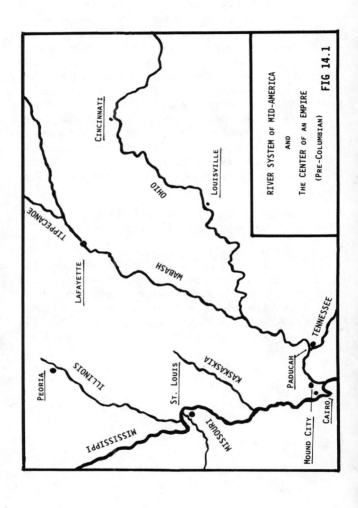

RIVER SYSTEM of MID-AMERICA
AND
THE CENTER OF AN EMPIRE
(PRE-COLUMBIAN)

FIG 14.1

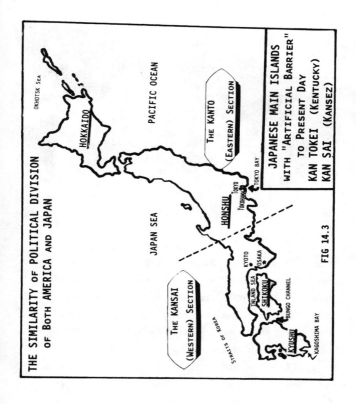

FIG 14.3

FIG. 14.3 ARTIFICIAL JAPANESE "BARRIER" SEPARATING
THE KAN TO FROM THE KAN SAI (EAST AND WEST OF BARRIER)
PARTS OF EARLY JAPAN. IN AMERICA, IT WAS THE GIANT
MISSISSIPPI RIVER THAT WAS "KAN, A BARRIER", GIVING
RISE TO KAN SEI (KANSEZ/KANSAS) AND KAN TO KEI (KENTUCKY).
KAN TO KEI WOULD BE THE ANCIENT CAPITOL CITY LOCATED
AT THE CAHOKIA MOUNDS OF ILLINOIS, ON THE EAST SHORE OF
THE MISSISSIPPI RIVER.

WITH NO NATURAL BARRIER OF RIVER OR MOUNTAINS, JAPAN
DENOTED AN ARBITRARY LINE OF DEMARCATION BETWEEN THE
CULTURAL CENTERS OF EAST AND WEST.

15. The Sun God Arrives In Japan

The early history of Japan is almost as much an enigma as that of the Americas. For while thousands of years a rich verbal language has flourished, it was not until about 2000 years ago that commerce and trade (with China) made it important for **Japan to develop a written language.** The languages of Japan and Korea are linked together, and are quite different from Chinese. In order to adopt a written language, it seemed convenient for the people of Japan to use the Ideographs that the Chinese traders used. These variations of "pictographs" conveyed entire thoughts or concepts, and were called KANJI characters (Fig.15.1).

While this satisfied a large part of the writing problems, still it found many of the sounds and conjugations needing supporting symbols. While the appearance of the characters were Chinese, their meanings were different, and certainly the pronunciation. They met this need with an alphabetic "phonetic system" called KANA, or Hiragana.

But where did their language come from? **Would such a small island nation develop a complex grammar language on its own, being so close to the developed Chinese nation.** Why were they not using Chinese? Why were they using a language that had spread throughout all of north America and most probably the two whole continents of the Americas as well? Perhaps you will say that it moved from Japan to the New World. Of course, I believe there is evidence for several migrations in both directions, but I feel linguistically there is evidence to speculate that the Language of the Americas arrived in Japan possibly along with the SUN GOD. I also see that a New World proto-language was being used. And later, politically, Japan would be divided up much as the ancient Empire of America had been divided! This was proposed in Chapter 14.

In Japan where the nobility resided in a place called Kashkoki, would it merely be a reflection of the origin of the expression as having been near an important river? Note that while these expressions appear in old Japanese dictionaries, they are not phrases ordinarily used by the young people of Japan today.

Is the morning greeting of OHAIYO GOZAIMASU actually an outgrowth of the Sun God greeting originating from atop the giant Mounds of Cahokia, Illinois as the Emperor or priests greeted the rising sun? The height of the mounds allowed them to be the first to greet the sun. Did the ceremony have the holy men or Emperor welcoming the sun as it breaks from the Eastern horizon in the direction of the New Day, "OHIO"?

We can conclude, however, that he was surrounded by his "nobility" at this point, for we see all the (present day Japanese) words for "NOBILITY, EMPIRE, RISING SUN, ABAN-

DONED MOUND, EAST and CAPITOL CITY" in this area. This is the area where these important Mississippi valley rivers such as Missouri, Ohio, Illinois, Tennessee and Wabash can be found.

Notice that two important sounds were in the Indian language that, if it went to Japan, became lost along the way. First, in Japan the "P" and "L" sounds were not used and the "TH" sound heard by the European explorers in America had become the "S" sound in Japan.

For example,

ALA BAMA would become ARU BAM'n

ARU KANSEZ would remain ARU KANSEZ
   (no change)

ILLO NOIE would become IRO NO

CULLONGE would become KURU ONGE

MUSKULLONGE would become MASU KURU
   ONGE

CHILLICOTHE would become (MI)CHI RI
   KASSEI

As noted by early explorers to America, the Indian language had an abundance of the W, U and O sounds, just as the language of Japan does today.

When the reign of the SUN GOD of Japan started approximately 2000 years ago, the Emperor system was directly a descendant of this god much as one can see in Central American history. The aborigine natives on the Japanese islands were conquered and a more monolithic society was close to being formed. The religion of

183

Shinto would be deeply based in worship of natural forces, love of outdoors and nature. This affection for nature would show up in their art and culture.

Even the deep signifiance of dreams (as in many societies) would be carried over within Japan where designated group members would be assigned the task. A whole group of southwest America Indians were involved with this culture. **Among them are a group called the YUMA, which is defined by the model as "Dream".**

Just as we have religious societies today in America that use snakes as part of their culture and worship, so did particularly those tribes of the Southwest Indians. While it has been reported that some tribes derisevely called other tribes "snakes" it may have been more accurately a reflection of their religious practices. Some Aztec dieties had the form of a feathered snake and the HOPI were widely known for snakes in their religious practice. **The word HOPI (modern HEBI) would mean "SNAKE"** in this re-construction of Indigo language.

By strange coincidence, then, these two important cultures used religious methods reflected in their very name given them by outside observers. The Nation called HOPI (today) itself is reported to mean "Peace", which must have reflected their own native meaning.[1]

A question might arise, did the language of the Algonquins reach out to the far West, to California, to the Baja? Definitely, yes! The language similarity between the American natives and that of simple early Japanese is evident. It appears from Eastern Canada to Mexico. There, in southern California is the tiny Indian village named Temecula. It is a place where early morning fog is well known. The translation shows it to be "divine or heavenly curtain", much as what is the old Indian recollection. Interestingly, this concept of fog is quite the way one of the chiefs at an upstate New York meeting of the 19th century metaphorically expressed his desire for good, sunny weather —"that Sun God should not cover himself with his garment".

Looking back at Chapter 13, we see a compilation of the historical events of Japan. The early aborigine (JOMON) natives were displaced by migrating and invading people. The influx of Asian (Mongolian) people came around 4000 BC. Then around 200 BC there was new pottery forms, called the YAYOI period and the introduction of warm-weather rice. (Cold-weather rice such as in America would wait for another 1000 years. Early rice suitable for cold climates had a different name, WASE—see WISCONSIN, Chapter 4).

About 239 AD the Japanese islands experienced an influx of people from the mainland, Korea and China. Shortly thereafter the ruling lords of Japan and their organization became quickly solidified. Shinto religion was introduced, based on natural elements and animals. Things and places had "holiness" (KAMI). The Sun God, AMATERATSU, was the first born of the gods that created the world and Japan. The political and military ruling clans laid claim to a divine representation of AMATERATSU through the great-great grandson JIMMU, the first earthly emperor. The divinity of the Emperor of Japan was launched, and would

185

flourish through many difficult eras terminating as we know, during this century (1946).

Shortly thereafter, about 400 AD the records show the movement of Buddhism to Japan from China. Also, at this time the pressing need for a written language was realized and this too was adapted from the Chinese. It was a period of change. Were there any special reasons for such a cultural revolution and political restructuring? Who were the people who invaded the islands in 239 AD? Were they nomadic hunting natives from the Americas or were they ex-patriates from the Empires of Mayan Mexico and South American Incas? Certainly the culture and language indicates a close relationship. The introduction of Shintoism and KAMI as a unique culture of these islands gives rise to the question of its similarity to those Indian religions of North America. The concept of "Holy places—KAMI" are widespread among the American natives.

The islands of ancient Japan carried the name, Country of the Sea Lion (ASHIHARA-NO KUNI). This animal some time later would become almost extinct — but not to worry, because the American natives had named ALASKA (ALIY ASHI KA) the same, and plenty of sea lions continued to live there. The island society developed feudal lords and a warrior society (SAMURAI). These aggressive "clans" were very much like the warrior groups developed in America. They even used the same names and expressions (based on model). The Samurai, like the Indians, considered themselves part of a clan, blood brothers. They were the UJI, blood brothers. This term most probably was derived from the expression, OJI-OBWA, meaning

"Uncle/Aunt people". (OJI-uncle and OBWA-aunt people). They also called themselves to be "the Way of the Bow and Arrow" during the 10th century AD.

This came as a pleasant surprise for when I had used the language model a few years earlier to translate the American Indian names of OJIBWA and ALGONQUIN, these are exactly what developed. (Ch. 4)

OJIBWA—(UJI)—Uncle/Aunt society, or Blood related clan or brotherhood.

ALGONQUIN—To Be of the BOW and ARROWHEAD (ARU KAN KUWAI'n)

It seems to be more than happenstance that these two great ancient social systems were linked together by similar vocabulary and culture.

The invading people entering Japan around the start of Christendom were mound-builders. These pyramid-like tombs called KOFUN were reported in some instances to have the bulk of the famous Egyptian ones. Population pressures in Japan have since destroyed much of these. This was called the YAMATO period, from which artifacts of the ruling class have been recovered. Similarly in America, many thousands of mounds have been located with many more overlooked. The largest and most impressive is near CAHOKIA in Illinois. (Ch.14).

The fact that a strong cultural and language relationship exists between the islands of Japan and the ancient peoples of America can not be much longer ignored. **By the study of todays Japan, I believe we can gain an inspiring and**

fulfilling insight into what Americas culture was before Columbus. This land was a challenge to the early natives. Some areas provided abundance, other areas tested to the limit the intelligence of these adaptable, flexible natives. The spirit MANITOU (MAN ITTO) utilized the highest order of multiple talents to guide, protect, and provide for the Indian. In many respects the American Indian culture was the antithesis to that of the encroaching Europeans. But, could it survive intact?

Can these studies at this point in time help define and distill these ancient cultures? As quoted before, one Indian leader said Americans have never understood the Indian. And under modern economic pressures, one might extend that opinion to say that Americans may never understand the Asiatic thinking either. But **by learning about one, we have a hope of finding the other.**

---

[1]*By model use, WABASH would be "People of Peace".*

AMERICA, LAND OF THE RISING SUN

KAN TO REGION (EAST OF BARRIER)

KAN SAI REGION (WEST OF BARRIER)

KANJI--- PICTOGRAMS OF
JAPANESE WORDS USING
CHINESE CHARACTERS.

BEI KOKU (RICE COUNTRY)

MICHI GAN (FLYWAY OF GOOSE)

美 国

BI KOKU (BEAUTIFUL COUNTRY)

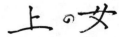

FIG 15.1   UE NO ONNA (FIRST BORN FEMALE-WINONA)

189

16. Mysteries Of Mexico, And Points South

Let us look at a modern happening: It was a happy time in a hospital along the California-Mexican Baja border. One of the many Japanese workers in America was celebrating the birth of their new baby in the maternity ward of this large hospital.

Some of the nurses from the Maternity section hurried excitedly down the hall and invited others into the ward to see the new baby. Not that the baby was in any way unique, other than being Japanese, but what surprised these young nurses was that **the baby had the MONGOLIAN SPOT.**

Other aides and nurses crowded around to see this purple-blue spot just above the tail-bone. It was only a matter of curiosity since the spot might disappear in three to forty months and was certainly not a real problem. Some pre-school teachers, however, having Japanese students for the first time suspected child abuse resulted in the bruise like pattern. And it may evoke questions from anthropologists.

For it was reported that this spot only appears on babies of Japanese heritage or Mexican Indians. Chinese and Korean babies do not have it. It is known in Japan as **the "Mongolian Spot"** but is also present in babies born in the islands of Guam or Saipan. It seems that as the original blood line is diluted below 25%, the new generations begin to lose the spot. Can this genetically linked occurrence offer any information to the student of Native American history? Why do we see this similarity? Let us look to history for what the AZTEC INDIANS of Mexico said.

A Four Hundred Year Old Puzzle—Solved At Last

It is an amazing story. The AZTEC Indians in Mexico had a rich and widespread empire. With natural curiosity, historians have documented their history (and mythology) with care. When asked by the Spanish who they were, they replied that they came from an island, AZTLAN, and it was far, far away.

From this description they became known as the AZTEC natives. But what does our model language do for us to solve this ancient puzzle? The suffix LA'n is common, meaning a specific place. So that place from whence they originated was AZT. First let us try to reduce the problem based on the Spanish and Portugese missionary[3] language. The originating place of these natives might be better written and pronounced as ASHILA'n where the Z has more of a "SHI" sound. Now it becomes fairly obvious that the island was "ASHILA'n—the Place of the Sea Lion—Ashi". This might be either islands off the coast of ALASKA (ALI ASHI KA—see Chap. 10) or more probable would be the islands of JAPAN

(ASHIHARA-NO-KUNI). Both describe ancient places of plentiful sea lions.

The AZTEC, however, also seem to have reported that ASHI was a lovely shorebird, the heron or crane. Indeed, the same word also means a pampa grass along the shores of Japan and a symbol of the country today is the crane (Japan Air Lines symbol). If we take the word of the Aztec literally, then, they were telling the Spanish that they were from Japan. They also were using ancient Japanese language, but their arrival in Mexico may have been relatively recent.

But why did they say they were ASHI-TEK (AZTEC)? Was there an ancient language which had the suffix "TEK" as meaning "WHERE I AM FROM"? Several groups of Mexico natives used the TEK suffix, the TOLTEC, MIXTEC, etc. Now we find what perhaps is a common link between all the American languages and those of northern Asia, and into the middle East. It is a common expression to use this suffix in languages linked to the ancient SUMERIANS and SCYTHIANS. The "TEK" suffix would mean literally "Where I am from". But that is beyond the topic of this book. Suffice to say that it strongly appears that the language found in the Americas and in Japan are both linked to a far more ancient language, the origination of which may have been in the Americas.

Shoes For The Children

Over the centuries, many Japanese children have been taught to weave sandals for work in the fields. These are made of reeds or straw such that they can work in rice fields and rainy weather with ease. **They are called WARAJI** with romanized spelling. But the sound of the word is the **same as the Mexican HUARACHES**. These Mexican Indian sandals are quite similar to their Japanese counterparts. Tourists familiar with the Japanese language who visit Mexico are amazed at the similarity in both name and product.

The Japanese people today call their more permanent footwear "KUTSU". And anything relating to the body could be "ME" as an archaic combination. ME-KUTSU would be "body shoe" which is the early word for North American Indian foot covering, "M'COTSU'n or **MOCCASIN**". Early explorers show the word to be best spelled as "M'COSUN" but it degenerated into the popular modern spelling.

If the Indians of Mexico are related in some way to the natives of Japan, we should also see a language relationship among the Mayan, Aztec and perhaps the Inca.

MEXICO—Land Of The EAGLE
On The CACTUS

When the Spanish explorers set off from their Caribbean base to explore the "mainland" they were directed to the rich country of MESHIKO (MEXICO). With the Conquistadors also came the Missionaries. Missionaries from the Spanish provinces had long travelled the earlier frontier areas of Africa. Conversion of natives to Christianity required understanding. That required a facility with language. They had evolved phonetics to interpret new sounds and language.

Because of this influence in Mexico many of the Indian names[3] were spelled in manners not easily comprehended by the English, much as the French influence along the Mississippi valley gave rise to various spellings of identical words.

MESHIKO was reported to mean the **"Center of Activity, a veritable Navel of activity"**. The center of this empire was at MEXICO CITY which **was called by the natives, "TENOCHTITLAN"**. Some accounts of this meaning propose it to be "Cactus eagle". This is based on the Aztec myth of its founding, at a place where an eagle would be seen on a cactus with a snake in its mouth. This is the legendary location that the Aztecs took as a holy sign to build their capitol city.

Of course, using the language model I propose, there is neither Cactus, snake, or eagle in the name for this most important Capitol city of the Aztec empire! It is more easily **translated to "Place of the People of the Empire of the SUN"**.

TENOCH—empire people

HI—rising sun, new day

LA'n—The specific place

For this was the city that would become MEXICO CITY, the center of trade, culture, and life for millions of followers or captives of the Empire.

The Empire was called MESHIKO (original sound) as some report. It also would be if the missionary phonetics are used where X is SHI. And more accurately interpreted, it indeed **does mean the CENTER of GROWTH ACTIVITY, or**

"Empire Navel". It seems that from the language, the navel or bud of a fruit was a most intriguing concept and meant "new life or divine and mysterious growth". Here it would be directly defined as: **"The Bud Starting Place"** or navel. Metaphorically speaking, it becomes:

ME—bud or young fruit

SHI—starting

KO,KA—place

From this reconstruction, the natives did not use a name for NAVEL, they just called it "beginning place"! Thus the professional linguist looking for the Nihongo "HESO" as being the interpretation for NAVEL would have a "fruitless search".

MIAMI, Another Center Of Activity

Quite a similar expression explains the several commercial activity areas used by the Indians in America. To anyone today looking at the fruits like the apple or orange, the vestigial blossom area of the "bud or navel" is quite obvious. The observations of sexual plant reproduction by these people, then, was by no means primitive. An area of new development could be called "the Bud of the Fruit—Miami." "ME is bud, MI is fruit or nut".

PERU—High In The Andes

Surprisingly then, the village high in the Andes mountains of Peru has a somewhat similar meaning. **It was named CUZCO, or a sound of KU SHI KO** where the I sound of SHI is almost silent as it is in Japan. Here the key variaton is that KU is "the Universe", and CUZCO would translate to: "The Universe Starting Place" which is the same as reported by the Peruvians speaking the QUECHUA language. It is said to mean **"the Belly Button of the World"**. Is the QUECHUA language similar to my proposed model of language? It has some instances of similarity and by applying the model a fascinating revelation is made of another famous city name.

The most holy city of the Incas ("hidden place") high in the mountains was not found by the Conquistadors. Much later it was discovered and its **name[1] was MACHU PICCHU**. Its name can tell us immediately why this city might have remained hidden from the Spanish invaders. It was not only a holy city of the Incas, but it BELONGED to the Inca Gods! And if it belonged to the Gods, this could explain why so many young women have been found buried there as probable sacrifices.

The model shows this city name to mean **"CITY BELONGING TO THE HEAVENS"**.

MACHU—city

BI,PI—belonging to

CHU—the Heavens

Of course, this might just be a strange coincidence that this language model developed for the North American Indians seems to fit so well even among the Meso-American Empires—even into South America. It does not surprise me. However, what does surprise me is that these similarities have not been brought more to the attention of the public, much of which has a keen interest in their history. It has been reported, however, in 1920 the Peruvian ambassador to Tokyo noted their strong language similarities and had written a book on it.

The Inca Mystery Of The Ancient Quipu

To administer to the Empire, the INCAS used a system that did not require writing. They kept "Tally strings" called QUIPU. The knots on the string were markers, to indicate obligations or quantities for the commercial or farming communities. These important items, called QUIPU are still used in Japan. They are **called the same, KIPPU,** and are tickets used at theatre or rail stations. Like any tickets which they are, they become tally markers indicating the obligation to provide an admission or a seat and may be traced to ancient INCA civilization, before writing was developed.

A similar system, it appears, was used by the ALGONQUIN of America. It was an allocation system to record debts and obligations called WAMPUM. WAPPU (like KIPPU) is the modern name in Japanese for an "allocation". In America, the English were not famous for accuracy in translating Indian words. The system as reported by early French was not "money" but only a way to record debt transactions. It later, however, took on the connotation of and was used as intrinsic trading value.

The Ancient Peruvian People

What kind of culture preceded the INCAS of Peru? Archeologists report that the MOCHE people were able to set up a farming civilization with irrigation a thousand years before the Inca. In fact, the terraces of farms along the mountainside gave the Spanish name "ANDE" ("terrace, platform") to the mountains. And the chain or "backbone" of mountains along South and North America was called the "CORDILLERAS" by the Spanish ("SEBO" by the Indian model). Without a written language they managed to administer a wide and complex society.

Today, many temples dot the Pacific shoreline with similar names as used by the Mississippi valley Indians thousands of miles north. We see the hybrid names of temples such as:

HUACA DEL BRUJO

HUACA DEL SOL

HUACA DE LA CRUZ

They are hybrid, adding the Spanish suffix to the native word for "temple — HUACA or WAKA". Indians of North America used this divine expression to denote their priests and holy places. It means by translation, "Divine understanding or knowledge". It could be a religious worship and resting place for mortal men. But reserved for the great GOD of the Sioux was "WAKA TEN KA" for this describes a spirit having "KNOWLEDGE AND UNDER-STANDING OF HEAVENLY PLACES". This was a task no mortal man could do. It is no coincidence that these far removed places and people were using a similar base language.

Just south of these temples is an entrance to a mountain valley. It is near here that the SANTA and VIRU rivers converge on their way to a fertile valley and the ocean. It was an important MOCHE site. It is called TANGUCHE. "TANI GUCHI" is a term for 'entrance or mouth of the valley' where the river can enter the sea.

A Study Of The Simple Life — Clothing Optional

The study of the Brazilian tribe of primitive natives called the YANOMOME brings a striking similarity to view. They run around naked in the jungle all day, leading a life the simplicity of which some of us might envy. Simplicity is their way of life, the bow and arrow their major weapon for food. Clothing for men and women is mostly non-existent. The major food is from the **Peach-Fruit Tree which they harvest and use for dowry value** in marriage liasons. It is interesting then to see in **"YANOMOME" the Japanese word for both FRUIT (Vegetable) and PEACH.** (YA-NO-MOMO).

Are these tribal people using a version of our language model as well? They, like most primitive groups, identify themselves as a Blood Brother society which they call "Uncle-Aunt", the very same nomenclature used by the OJIBWA Indians of Canada. Another most interesting sidelight to their tribal name is that it also is another (current) way of saying "People of the Arrow" (YA NO MONO). This is what the OJIBWA proclaimed themselves to be, the **ALGONQUIN, "to be of the Bow and Arrowhead". (ARU KAN KUWAI'n).**

HISTORY IS QUICKLY RECEDING

It has been less than 500 years ago that vast invasions from Europe left confusion among our native dwellers. **We must clarify the American heritage soon.** If not, it will be forever lost in the dust of endless new armies of people marching through this window of time that each will call "today". If a model of this ancient verbal language can help to shed new light on these ancestors of the "NEW WORLD", then we should welcome it. We should tune it, as one would a fine musical instrument, to extract from the instrument a harmonius **understanding of these great civilizations never before enjoyed.**

For the ancient language may not be dead, its mutant form could be alive and well and saved for us in Japan. It would be in the form of a modern "high-level" language which we need only to dissect and reassemble, much as can be done with assembly language computer software.[2]

[1] *Actually, the city of Machu Picchu was reported as named after the mountain upon which it rested. It was said to mean "Old Mountain". Nearby was another tall mountain called* **HUAYNA PICCHU (UE NA BI CHU)**. *Based on model translation,* **this is the mountain** *which means "Elder or Old, belonging to the Heavens". It appears to have been confused with Machu Picchu sometime between antiquity and the present. There are other "Heavenly mountains". In Alaska. Mt. McKinley had the* **native name of "DENALI",** *which would mean "to be in the Heavens or clouds—TEN ALI". Or a possible "To be the stairway to the Heavens" using the expression for temple steps, "DON".*

[2] *While a computer data base helps immensely with cataloging word sounds, more sophisticated mathematical techniques of recovering ancient language has not yielded results. The* **very nature of primitive language,** *the metaphors, the poetic license of interpreters, and dialects* **produces a GIGO situation** *(garbage in-garbage out) that reduces the probability that new exotic techniques using computers would be entirely successful.*

[3] *See Chapter 4 for the Language influence of missionaries.*

17. I'll Take Manhattan

I'll take Manhattan, and any other prime oceanside properties.—That may be the popular song of the Japanese investor today if he has the old spirit, Manitou (**"Wisdom or talent of the First Order of Magnitude"**). **The North American Indians relied on Manitou to provide for and guide them.**

It is a bit of historical irony that some of the landmark buildings of New York's Manhattan island may be bought up by Japanese investors. After a couple thousand years are these the remote descendents or cousins of the American Indian returning to these sacred grounds. Returning to the island of Manhattan where the spirit Manitou has been completely forgotten, his teachings and spirit almost the antithesis of the prevailing materialistic psychosis? Real estate, it seems, has taken on modern values among the Japanese who have sustained themselves on such small islands in the Pacific.

A question which may be of little importance but evokes much curiosity is often asked, "If ancient American and Japanese civilizations are so much similar, in which direction was there a movement? Actually, it is evident from language that both directions of migration have been used at different times. The abundance of the sea lion along Alaska appears to have at one period triggered a recent migration. And political unrest in

Mexico territory may have precipitated a migration to Japan 2000 years ago. Based on Aztec legend, they returned from Japan (AZTLAN)[1] in recent times, perhaps around 900 AD. In 1325 the beginnings of the great Capitol of TENOCHTITLAN (now Mexico city) were started. By 1428 the Aztec Empire was reigning supreme just in time to "welcome" the Spanish Conquistadores.

Much earlier than this, however, it would appear evident that a proto-language existed similar to that in both Japan and the Americas. This will be discussed later.

We might ask if there were other early migrations of aborigines or natives from Japan that settled into the Americas, bringing a specific philosophy of life and language from the Orient? Or had there been an early movement from Africa, from the Mediterranean coasts that brought a middle East language to these shores? A language that then moved into the Japanese islands.

With a language similarity between primitive America and Japan, it might provide less of a cultural shock to the travelling Japanese business man of modern day. Twenty-six states in America, for instance, have names derived from Native American descriptions using words that are almost modern Japanese. From this point of view, many more of Americas names of Indian heritage may become obvious to the Japanese. Words such as:

SHIAWASSEE river—in Michigan (Happy river)

WEEKIE WACHI—home of alligators, floating
    (UEKI)

YOSEMITE— valley between mountains in
    California

SYRACUSE—in New York

TONAWANDA—in N.Y.

GOWANDA —near the 5 finger lakes of N.Y.
    (GO WAN)

All derived verbally from early Indian locations.

Island Mentality—A Sort Of Kangaikatte

One of the burning problems in the economy of
the world is "Trade Balance". It is probably of
most concern to small nations and certainly to
those island nations having limited natural
resources, such as Japan. What develops, I see, is
what may be called an **"ISLAND MENTALITY"**.
It is a way of thinking (the Japanese call it KAN-
GAIKATTE) **that is forced upon islanders** because of necessity—because their future and
fortune are solely their own problems to solve.
There is no larger entity or resource to bail out
errant performance. It's DO or DIE.

Some classic economic problems can be
reduced to "how will it work on an Island?". We
all have heard the explanation of the novice
businessman, "I lose a nickel each, but I plan to
make it up on volume". If it won't work in a small
situation, if it can't work on an island, it won't
work in a larger setting. It will just become apparent sooner to the economic or political structure constrained by a smaller shoreline. **For all
nations are islands**, it's only the size and nature

of the borders that are different. If a small island economy can not afford deficient fiscal policies, then neither can a larger one — but it may take longer to become apparent.

I earnestly feel that the Japanese businessman feels more comfortable with "island mentality" than his American counterpart. He may also feel more comfortable doing business in America than his counterpart does selling in Japan. One reason might be the somewhat familiar Indian language of American states and landmarks. Or it might be a natural nomadic tendancy to think on a more large, global scale — quite the opposite which one might expect from an island nation. Particularly one that had practiced such intense isolationism up until the mid-1800's. How did this island mentality suddenly explode into global economic and technical, let's say, **activity — if not domination?**

At this point you might be looking for a specific answer. I can point to the heritage of these small islands in the light of what has been revealed and developed. What historians could be faced with is a complex but highly active entity of the Americas and a specific relation to Asia heretofore overlooked.

Unwritten history is particularly difficult to reconstruct and we owe a large debt to the professional archaeologists and anthropologists who have painstakingly developed for us an almost vivid view of our American artifacts on two continents. With further development, these language revelations will help us to firm up our view of this heritage as well as the history of the Japanese islands.

What we may have once seen as primitive societies in the Americas (South, Meso and North) can turn out to be a "mother-lode" of culture which spread out over vast areas, even into Asia. Whatever the background, I feel that these strong language similarities between the Americas and present day Japan make for a very unique history of development for that island nation! The people founding the Japanese dynasties were strong in will and culture. If, as this study suggests, that the founders of what we might call modern Japan (after 100 AD) were originally from the Americas, then it can explain the unique, dynamic nature of this society, a society basically quite unlike the ancient Chinese.

These "colonists" from America brought with them a heritage of nature, dedication, and a culture very obsessed with the SUN GOD. Their heritage was the SUN EMPIRES of Meso and South America. It may have been a quiet invasion, almost peaceful as these rather taller colonists met the diminutive YAYOI or JOMON natives. When the sea lion disappeared from Japan, they started a journey back to North America, along the Alaskan coast.

Recent Anthropology Results

Studies by Prof. Turner at Arizona[2] reported a unique intermix of dental characteristics among Asians in old archaelogical finds. Some work was done in Japan several years ago. These indicated that there are two distinct types of tooth structure among the Asian peoples. One of the types (sinodonty) is found among the more northerly east Asiatic people. These are reported by him to be the Chinese, Mongols, Buryats, modern Japanese, eastern Siberians as well as all the original native inhabitants of the Americas. His data supports possible movements by Asian people into America 15,000 years before the present. This is even more interesting inasmuch as many of these seem to have also been using the same proto-language.

Human language is unique among the mammals of the world. And it is durable. It has been said that it is more difficult to kill off a language than a people and culture themselves. And then parts of the language arise among surviving victors.

Dr. Loring Brace (Univ. of Michigan)[3] reported distinct skull differences between the general Japanese and that of the "nobility or ruling class". This class bears a stronger relationship to the northern AINU, often associated with strong resemblances to American Indians. Here again is shown two distinct anthropological backgrounds with the Nobility Class and Samurai having structure more in line with that of the American Native. The proposed theory of some Japanese anthropologists that their history had been studded with several foreign inclusions can lead to some very interesting conjecture. So what we find here is not the monolithic society the Westerner might be led to believe and expect. Modern Japan might be more accurately compared to the Atom, fueled by a nucleus of protons, neutrinos, electrons, quarks, etc. Has it been the MIDWIFERY of the American natives thousands of years ago that has contributed to the birth of this highly unique and successful nation?

Some may ask what good are studies such as these. Aside from the everpresent academic curiosity among scholars, it is most interesting for families to know their heritage. In one sense, it is sometimes comforting for an adopted child to find he has cousins, maybe brothers. And if, by these studies, the native American Indians find they have long-forgotten cousins practicing a similar culture and language on a distant island, springing up like the spirit MANITOU from that island to become a global force in technology and economics, then that may be a benefit. Just as Alex Haley provided "ROOTS" for his people, maybe this study will in some way give substance to the tantalizing but nebulous history of Americas native people.

And for the American business executive, possibly he should study MANITOU and listen to the divine winds whispering through the wilderness from Wisconsin to New York. "MANITOU, the WISDOM and LEARNING of the FIRST MAGNITUDE" then is not limited to the benfit of the Indian. All should remember, the Machi Manitou (wrong talents) can also mislead the greedy and unwary. He will quickly find that greed, avarice and malpractice are not the foundations of empire. The many talents and flexibility of this Indian Spirit might be an example from which all can learn. The Dutch, when encountering the spirit filled Indian island in New Amsterdam harbor, pronounced it MANHATTAN (MANITOU'n).

The island lives, but perhaps the spirit has died.

[1] See Chap. 16: The Aztecs reported they came from an island far away, a place called AZTLAN. This would be translated by our language model to "Place of the Sea Lion —ASHI LA'n". This was the ancient name for the Japanese Islands (Brinkley: Japan/English Dictionary).

[2] Scientific American, Feb. 1989: "TEETH AND PREHISTORY in ASIA" by Christy G. Turner II, Arizona State Univ.

[3] Am. Journal of Physical Anthropology and NYT News Service; San Diego Union 6-26-90. C.Loring Brace of Univ. of Michigan.

18. Targeting Of America

America Never Listened To The Indian

The historical details of our American continents are interesting to learn and study. But, **more importantly**, how can this history relate to the perspective of our world today, a world of increased trade and communications? Can it help us understand and evaluate the cultures of pre-Columbian America and the Japanese culture of the same period? And most important, can the information learned about cultural similarities and differences be used to **help direct American understanding and policies to becoming more socially and economically effective?**

For several years after mid-20th century, there has been an acute awareness of "America International". We had been a nation emerging from the charitable Marshall Plan into becoming a world player in the **highly competitive game of "money and technology"**. At the birth of this new era, America's industrial management was like an adolescent poker player with **a handful of all the right cards**.

Much of the wartime development and research (from both sides of the combat) that had been directed towards new technologies was available to industrial executives and government planners. Like the fountainhead (MINNESOTO) or spring (WAUKESHA) that gushed from the ground, **it was an artery of wealth** that need only be tapped into. One of the most important areas of new development was, of course, Electronics.

Here was a stage upon which infinite innovation could be performed—from complex Radar to the simplest battery operated toy or radio. Television emerged as a social necessity to many millions of families. The technology to perform most of these miracles had been underwritten in the years before in the laboratories of Europe and America.

One had only to tap into this mainstream of know-how and be flexible enough to divert it into profitable products. While it had been customary for years to power these products from a power line cord, the advent of the low voltage transistor would soon make possible a host of new products and toys that would not need specific approval by public safety institutions. Result—anyone could play the game. And America had, it appeared, a bottomless market demand for all types of goods. It opened a literal flood-gate to the importation of electronic devices at varying levels of sophistication.

TARGETING is a term often used. Management of industrial empires try to use it—often targeting for goals of short term financial return and growth. Less often, it seems, there has been targeting of important world markets for a product having high commercial value. Look, for instance, at the IBM product and success story. There is nothing wrong with targeting. Especially if you are shooting the arrow! It gets tiring when you are the "javelin catcher". The Japanese businessman can rightfully say that "target" is our name. The old name for Japan, YA-MATO, could be interpreted as "Arrow Target". And the new name, NIP-PON, still has the American Indian name, NIP, for "arrow".

American business has long been criticized by observers in Japan for a lack of long term vision, a lack of flexibility in dealing with problems. Those American industries such as IBM and Motorola showing this capability of vision often also show the successes. However, those successful industries manipulating large monopolized supplies of natural resources or markets can not be looked upon for guidelines. It is the business of everyday production of wealth against **competitive forces of the world** where the true value of good management can be seen. And this takes **Dedication, Obligation, and Innovation**.

Not too much different from what the settlement of the Americas required of early pioneers, both Indian and European.

But what is the production of wealth? America has been a wealthy nation by several standards. Wealth, as reported by economics, is concerned with production not service. Production of national wealth is attained by producing three things: goods of manufacture, commodities of agriculture, or raw materials from mining.

As on a small island, prosperity is not gained by you shining my shoes, and me yours. You can not produce wealth for a nation through trading internal services. You may encounter people ob-

213

jecting to this as they personally know service workers, insurance agents or entertainers who are wealthy. But they are often consumers of wealth, not creators. Manufacturing jobs can create the "most jobs per dollar sold" and are often at the backbone of a successful economy.

The "trickle down" effect of money used in manufacturing has been amply demonstrated. Many remember the active state-wide economies that have been tied like a shoestring to the huge automotive industry that America enjoyed for so many years. States like OHIO, ILLINOIS, INDIANA, MICHIGAN, WISCONSIN all enjoyed a large share of trickle down prosperity from Detroit. It created JOBS.

The importance of labor and manufacturing appears to be appreciated by most emerging countries and has been essentially forgotten by government leaders of America. Are we becoming a supplier of raw materials and importer of high technology goods? These are the marks of a third-rate country, in fact, a colony. You would have to rationalize your thinking to deny this trend. Is it that American leaders, as often perceived by Japanese executives, are too engulfed in other conflicts to properly target the main problem.

These conflicts range from self-interest, unemployment, civil rights, race relations, drug abuse, and policing the world. The "problems" are admittedly real, but how many of them would disappear if our economy were basically strong and healthy and everyone that wanted a meaningful job could have one?

Young people today often refer to a basic feeling, ATTITUDE, and it can be at the very bottom of our problem. Perhaps we should listen to what successful foreign marketing entities have assessed our problems to be. Certainly a nation with such a rich history and with the capability for world-wide respect must re-asess it's priorities when faced with problems as destructive as the present day economic situation of too many drugs and too few jobs.[1]

We must have an attitude—one of understanding and listening. Once we have that, the planning and action should become obvious. Long ago, one of the complaints of an Indian tribal chief was that American government did not listen to them, nor did they ever really understand America or the Indian. Do our elected government representatives today **really understand our American history and our present problems and solutions?** Perhaps, in some small way, this new perspective of history in America and Japan may help adjust our thinking.

The once flourishing electronic industry in America can act as a weather vane to tell us which way the wind is blowing. (Do we really need to pay a government Weatherman to tell us everything is OK). We can essentially say, "America is no longer the industrial fountainhead for innovation". The torch will be passed to nations that have governing people who are able to effectively plan and guide. We can not blame "government", only the "people of government". We can all accept that responsibility. If this torch is passed to others, it will be another sad chapter in Americas misunderstanding and misplaced benevolence. It

215

is the obligation of democratic people to keep their delegates honest and their "toes in the fire".

Like the aging businessman who hires the young man to shine his shoes, then do his book-keeping, call on customers, and manufacture the products. He soon finds he must rely entirely on his "partner" and someday soon he himself will be out of the business. World wealth is in products of technology and jobs and personal wealth belongs to those who help propagate them, not manipulate them.

One dominant historical fact continues to surface in the study of the Americas and their **ancient people—technology, or more importantly, the lack of it.** Isolation on the early continents of America separated the highly intelligent natives from advances in modern metal-working and transportation. Without animals of burden such as mules or horses, there was little need to develop the wheel as long as the nations had abundant waterways for large canoes. The lack of steel and modern weapons provided a backdrop for **the demise of native civilization**. The use of these technologies for political dominance was vital to the European expeditions which followed the Columbus discoveries. The vital development by the Indians of the flint arrowhead was self-proclaimed progress—but it was no match for the guns and horses of the expeditionaries.

History And Mythology

Mythology is an important part of all civiliza-tions. It was particularly important to the primi-tive peoples where no written accounts were made. Even today, mythology is of passing interest to many who are entertained by mystic numbers or the astrology charts of newspapers and periodicals. And there are those like Joseph Campbell[2] who contributed a lifetime to recording and analyzing the worldwide effect of various mythologies upon our culture. Can it be that most such myths are not whimsical, but represent some specific event or truth that the culture wishes to perpetuate down to future civilizations?

Of the many mythologies of the Native Americans, one is of particular interest. It sought to establish a perspective on the Indian civilization and its future. Ironically, it foretold of the Indian losing his homeland—being driven out. But this would not be the end, for as the story was related, in time this **intruder, too, would lose these lands**.

Is this a prophecy which could happen to America—or was it a prophecy fulfilled with the Spanish invasion and expulsion from the Sonora and New Mexican territories? If it is a mythical prophecy of substance, then how could the occupants of these great nations in some way lose them? Through military conflict or through financial manipulation? We need only look to the worlds map-makers to understand that political borders are certainly less than permanent. Can we look forward to the day when there are happily no more restrictive boundaries?

Assuming that the prophecy can become true, it is interesting to speculate if it could be a financial invasion from Asia that will consumate the prophecy?

Or could it be a gigantic environmental or geological disaster? A disaster which would drive all Americans back to the sacred land. It would be the historical Land of Manitou which the white man, until now, never did understand, and the Indian understood so well.

---

[1]*Perhaps the problem of jobs and drugs is more closely related than previously addressed. Certainly there are many areas where the immediate financial rewards of drugs creates employment opportunities no where else available. And if challenging jobs for all were available, might there be no time nor need for recourse to stimulants?*

[2]*Joseph Campbell, popular author and historian specializing in world mythologies.*

19. The Tribal Village

A Close Look at The VILLAGE

The world today is getting ever smaller. Actions and reactions by peoples on opposite sides of the earth have a tendency to reverberate back and forth giving effects much like an earthquake, and sometimes as destructive. The average person today can see, if he looks, four large political bodies each holding a large amount of economic power or potential. These countries are Japan, USA, China and USSR. And looming on the horizon is the European common market. It's as though everyone is getting ready for a good economic ballgame.

It can be a little unsettling to the thoughtful American family to see and realize what the world economic figures can mean. First, one should not overlook the strange lineup of the batting order above. In the statistics of land-mass there is one maverick in the lineup—Japan, with not much more land than the state of California. But take a look at **the startling economic figures of the Japanese Empire and world trade:** [1]

International Banking

- The 20 largest Banks in the World, 13 are Japanese
- The 10 largest Banks in the World, 8 are Japanese
- The 8 largest Banks in the World, 8 are Japanese

The 20 largest Public Companies:

1	NTT	Japan
2	Industrial Bank	Japan
3	IBM	USA
4	Sumitomo Bank	Japan
5	Dai-Ichi Kangyo Bank	Japan
6	Fuji Bank	Japan
7	Mitsubishi Bank	Japan
8	Exxon	USA
9	Royal Dutch/Shell	Dutch
10	Toyoto Motors	Japan
11	Tokyo Electric	Japan
12	Sanwa Bank	Japan
13	General Electric	USA
14	Nomura Securities	Japan
15	AT&T	USA
16	Nippon Steel	Japan
17	Matsushita Elec.	Japan
18	Hitachi	Japan
19	Philip Morris	USA
20	Tokai Bank	Japan

Japanese Investments In Metropolitan Areas

In $ Millions

Area	1988	1989
Los Angeles	$3049	$2512
New York	2802	2304
San Diego	421	1103
Honolulu	1325	1064
Anaheim	506	621
Las Vegas	22	482
San Francisco	740	358
Wash. DC	638	356
Houston	60	300
Phoenix	140	280
other Met	6182	1691
other Non-met	659	3703
Total	$16,544	$14,775

(source: Kenneth Leventhal & Co.)

Appearing in San Diego Union Newspaper, 6-24-90

This is not being critical of the International situation, for interdependant commerce is a cornerstone of modern economies. It is politically important as well. This merely shows the apparent strength of such a small producer nation. It is like a baseball scorecard—in the 7th inning. You can see who is winning.

But International business is not a game. There must be no losers and winners in the long run. All "islands and tribal villages" must survive, and if possible, prosper.

A Quick Look At Symptoms

An old adage reflected the thought that it didn't take a weatherman to tell one which way the wind was blowing. The electronic technology employment market has been virtually destroyed in USA. However, America does have a much higher ratio of Lawyers to Engineers than Japan. Perhaps that is symptomatic of our village problems. While American government officials are lauding the fact that more jobs are created in America each year, they would have to be mental midgets to deny the fact that:

➤ Jobs should normally increase as population grows.

➤ The Jobs generated are nowhere near the type of product manufacturing and engineering which are needed to support an advanced technical economy.

➤ The Service Industry and raw materials growth are the indicators of a Third world country, not a leading Power! Imports of high tech products and export of agriculture and raw materials are not the hallmark of a progressive economic power.

The Tribal Village

Let us not jump to blame other countries for the economic and social problems that we see now and in the future. It most probably can be said that the problems were "MADE IN USA".

It may have appeared to the primitive hunter that large animals were not vulnerable to the spear or arrow. He certainly became quickly aware that the new FLINT ARROWHEAD could pierce the buffalo hide. But he also knew that a little blood loss from a single arrow might end up fatal to these large animals. The continual bleeding of a rich economy, the extraction of its investment wealth through needless taxation as well as benevolently spreading abroad the fruits of its expensive technology can produce an anemic industrial carcass that earns no world respect.

The TRIBAL VILLAGE envisioned early in this century by people like Huxley and McLuhan is a heritage left to and squandered by America. **The ethics to insure tribal survival left America**—but not to worry! It had been transported two thousand years before and was safely cached away in the islands of Japan. As a butterfly from a cocoon, it would when the time was right, emerge as a glamorous enigma to confound the American economists. That time came after World War II.

Feeding on the nectar of self-indulgent American administrators, the world butterflies congregated around one of the largest consumer markets the world had ever seen. We can not blame any outside sources for doing what, if permitted, we would do ourselves. The public officials may have had little long term concept of what they were doing.

We are living in an age of Technology, an age of Information. Our employment, according to one source, is now engaged 55% doing work in Information. Another 15% do work in other personal service fields. That doesn't leave many to work in the backbone of "wealth production", that of product manufacturing. The industries of manufacturing produce the highest amount of "trickle-down" jobs and real "village wealth".

The World Tribal Village is getting smaller. Jobs and **work ethics** are at the basis of any successful village, no matter how big or important that village appears to be. A healthy village can not export jobs for long, nor should it want to. It would appear that somewhere in the past, **America and Japan shared a rich, tribal heritage**. But the enjoyment of our present economic relations leaves a lot to be desired—not condemned.

The Aztec story of flexibility and re-birth is inspiring.[3] The Empire of the Sun was an important American theme a thousand years ago. Let us finally understand AMERICA and move ahead from there, **a productive and prosperous member of the TRIBAL VILLAGE, with an ISLAND MENTALITY** — realizing "What we don't do for ourselves, we cannot expect others to do for us without a cost".

[1]*from the Wall St. Journal, dated 9-22-89*

[2]*from Financial Focus report by Morgan Stanley Capitol Int.*

[3]*Lost Empires, Nat. Geographic; 1982 pg.124 The story of the Aztec people relates how defeat forced them to surrender. They were relegated by the Calhua chief to the worst lava area inhabited by many snakes. Instead of succumbing, they ate the snakes and prospered. Serving their masters well, they even married into the Calhuas. But, after sacrificing a Calhuan princess, they were chased out to a swampy area of lake Texcoco. They then realized an important fact, that no one wanted this swampland. They built the marsh up into land and built canoes. They began maritime trading from their watery headquarters. After several years they commanded the lake areas and were able to form alliances which would put them in control of the entire empire. In 1325 they would form their capitol, TENOCHTITLAN, the head of the Empire of the Sun.*

FIG 19.2

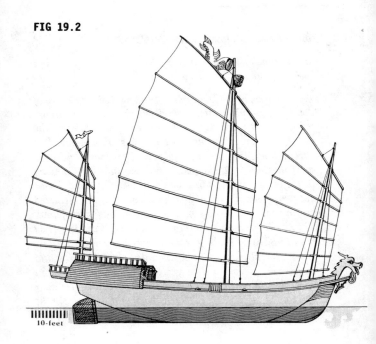

10-feet

NU SUN'S SHIP ca. 550 B.C.
This is an artist's conception of the design of Nu Sun's expedi-
tionary vessels, which sailed from China to Meso-America ca.
500 B.C. The vessel was probably an adaptation of an existing
ship design that was ancestral to the Canton seagoing junk.
Cloth sails may have been an early design feature borrowed from
Phoenician merchants. Approximate length: 70-80 feet.

DRAWINGS COURTESY GUNNAR THOMPSON, "NU SUN": PIONEER PUBLISHING
2350 E. GETTYSBURG AVE. FRESNO, CA. 93726

226

20. Questions And Controversy

Approaching the languages of these American civilizations from this new viewpoint can raise questions. Some of these questions and controversy raised by various readers are addressed.

The Navajo Code-Talkers

A question often brought up by people who study the history and rich accomplishments of the American natives is the wartime communications legend of the Navajo. Their language was considered quite unique by the military so they were put into action for coded communication purposes.

In the Pacific theatre of operations during WW II several groups of the Navajo used their native language to send messages of military intelligence over the radio. Of course, additionally, locations and key information were further encrypted. This was reported to be a quick but effective method to send security messages over the air, without being de-coded by the Japanese listening posts.

In the light of this new information on language similarity, the question arises as how this could be successful? The language group of the Navajo is reported to be related to the Algonquin which in turn is here shown to be closely coupled to recent

Japanese. First, I'm not sure it was completely secure. It is not something, like the American breaking of the Murasaki (Purple) Code, to be talked about. However, like any dialects or language, it would take a long time to recover the unwritten language before any crypto-analysis can be done on the information content. American native speakers who have listened regularly to Japanese language at prison camps report that it has a very familiar and comfortable rhythm and inflection but they have no way to "understand" the language. And that probably works both ways.

Columbus And His Doubts

On board the ships of original voyage of Columbus, was a trader of Arabic/Hebrew background. It was foresight that brought him along on such an adventurous trip. Columbus, realizing that if he were successful, he would need to exchange communications with the Chinese lords and emperors. In preparing for this trip, accounts from Marco Polo of 200 years before were studied, and the rich islands off the Chinese shore were of immense interest. These were named by Marco Polo as CIPANGO (JIPANGO—JAPAN).

When the Caribbean islands were reached, it must have been a somewhat confusing puzzle. For, I am sure, had the Arabic interpreter listened to the people, he would have felt safe to say they had landed close to the Japanese islands. And just beyond these islands, according to reports by Marco Polo, were the mainlands of China and India. Yet, somehow, everything did not yet fit together—where were the Emperors, the Gold Palaces, and the adornments of silk? This would soon be answered, but Columbus would not live to see the Empires of Mexico and Peru discovered (and exploited). On one of his trips, as his grasping for the empires seemed to elude him, he came up with what today seems like a modern idea— SPREAD THE BLAME!

The Orient seemed so tantalizing close on each of his previous trips that he must have felt a frustration of immense proportions. A type of frustration typical when faced with overwhelming clues and little confirmation, handicapped by ancient communication and navigation systems. One must remember that while latitude can be easily measured, the distance between continents (longitude) depends heavily upon an accurate time base. This would be lacking for another 50 years. It is said that he finally wrote a verification that it was the opinion that his ships had indeed reached close to the China shores. He then asked all of his crew to sign this declaration, which for the most part, they did.

Today, in the bright light of hindsight, it is easy to empathize with the frustrations of this bold man, Columbus. We can see why in desperation he wanted to assure the Spanish Crown that it was not he alone who had come to such a justifiable but puzzling conclusion. Although he could not wholly understand it, it was the only conclusion he could make, given the language and lifestyle reports being delivered to him.

Other Languages In America

Some students of American language have observed indications of many (European) languages among the Indian place-names. I am sure this can be explored more fully if we can "distill" out the ones which are obviously non-conforming. Some of the language similarities reported are Norwegian, Welch, Irish, Libyan, Arabic. If, as these studies show, there is a layer of ancient nomadic language across the northern lattitudes of the world, then we would expect to see residue from many languages.

The Norwegian diminutive suffix is "OSIS" which you might expect to see in place names. America is abundant with "little" being appended to many lakes and landmarks. The great lake in Canada, WINIPEG, has also a smaller sister lake, WINIPEGOSIS. Could this be a hybrid between Norwegian and Japanese (UE NO BEIKO OSIS) meaning "Little lake of Superior Wild Rice". If this is true, then how does it place Norwegians (Vikings) so far into Canadian territory of Manitoba? There are many questions to be answered.

American Genetics —
A Common Ancestral Group

Recent work on DNA ancestral coding has revealed some interesting proposals. Present reports seem to show that the natives of South and North America share mitochondrial genes (from Female) of only a small number of women. Thus, it would seem to confirm the theory that they could all have started with a similar language. The work done by Wallace of Emory University is revealing. This is exactly where the studies here lead to[1]. Not only one language, but **that language seems to be an early nomadic language** of Euroasia that also settled into the Japanese islands. It appears to have been quite similar to a language used by the ancient Scythians or Sumerians, and Huns. Was it a language that had developed in the Americas and spread across Asia? Most views are that it moved into the Americas, but that can be debatable. We can, of course, see recent importation of Asiatic language into the Americas.

Ancient Writing In America

Here is a topic of importance and disappointment. An aura of suspicion is often cast over these findings because of earlier charlatans and counterfeiters. Based on these studies, there seems to be every reason to find evidence of early World languages written among the stones of the New World. Appendix A reveals some probable forms of early writing which might be encountered. Since the Language of the Americas developed here seem to be closely linked to early Sumerian and Scythian peoples, we should also find traces of their primitve writing.

Summary

There was an ancient LANGUAGE of the AMERICAS. It appears to be revealed in these pages showing meanings and grammar having overwhelming congruency to an archaic language. That language would appear to be the proto-language to both the Japanese and to the American natives. It pre-dates written language. It bears a resemblance to what might be reconstructed as that of Scythian or earlier cultures, those that also moved into and developed the ancient Sumeria and middle east. Further study and research will certainly confirm that an ancient language permeated much of the planet. The power and mobility of early nomadic "empires" might assume proportions never before imagined. They moved with environmental demands, they left little that we could call cities and artifacts. But their travels and knowledge were spread across the earth. Then there was a general settling of these nomads, and we see the beginnings of civilization as we think of it. And many parts of this ancient language, like fossilized artifacts, are still with us today.

---

[1] *According to anthropological geneticist Steven Zegura of the University of Arizona, based on genetics a possibility of a very limited number of ancient language migrations between the Americas and Asia is quite probable.*

AMERICA, Land Of The Rising Sun

APPENDIX A
Writing Of Runic And Etruscan

Tracing the early writings of civilizations has been an intriguing adventure and many scholarly hours have been spent on it. Verbal language precedes the written words by many thousands of years and is more difficult to recover from history. Writing is a somewhat recent invention of man.

Coupled with technology, writing would act as a catalyst to ignite and propel civilization ahead at high speed. Pictographs were a natural place to start, but the phonetics (used by Phoenicians) were a giant leap to record concepts.

Shown here are alphabets used in ancient records. They are the type which are readily inscribed in clay or wood with a sharp instrument.

It shows the similarity between language of ancient Hungarian and Etruscan.

A Comparison of Ancient Alphabets

Ancient Hungarian

Etruscan

Magyar

Etruszk

Ancient Hungarian

Etruscan

(FADRUSZ, J.)

AMERICA, Land Of The Rising Sun

Appendix B — Bibliography

The McKenney-Hall Portrait Gallery of American Indians by James D. Horan; Bramhall House, N.Y., 1972

The American Heritage Book of Indians by editors of American Heritage; by American Heritage Publishing, Bonanza books; 1988

The Book of the Samurai, the Warrior Class of Japan by Stephen R. Turnbull; Gallery Books WH SMITH,N.Y.

Touch the Earth by T.C.McLuhan; Promontory Press, N.Y.1971

The Indians' Book, recorded and edited by Natalie Curtis Bonanza Books, N.Y. 1987

The World of the American Indian by Nat. Geographic Society; by NGS Publishing 1974

The Sioux People of the Rosebud by Paul Dyck; Northland Press, Flagstaff,AZ; 1971

Gateway to Empire by Allan W. Eckert;Bantam Books, N.Y.;1983

The History of the Lewis and Clark Expedition by Elliott Coues,editor Volumes 1, 2, and 3 with Maps; Dover Publications,Inc. N.Y.; original 1893 by Francis P. Harper

The OLD WEST , The INDIANS by TIME LIFE BOOKS, New York 1973. reprinted 1976.

These United States, by READERS DIGEST , 1968; published by Western Publishing Co.

LOST EMPIRES, Nat. Geographic 1982 Wash D.C.

Invitation to Linguistics, by Mario Pei H.
Regnery Co. Chicago; 1965

Origins of Language, by James Ludovici; G.P.Putnams
Sons; N.Y. 1965 Cong#: 65-10870

**Pictorial Encyclopedia of American History 1450 -
1733**; Vol. 1, Davco Pub. Co. Chicago 1962

The American Heritage Vol.1, New WORLD by Robert
Athearn; Dell Publishing Co. N.Y.
(American Heritage Magazine);1963

LANGUAGE, editors Clark, Eschholz,
Rosa St.Martens Press NY 4th Edition 1985

THE DEATH AND REBIRTH OF THE SENECA by
Anthony Wallace pub. by Alfred A. Knopf, Inc.
1970 (Random House)

**A NEW WORLD TO CONQUER, Vol. of "The Story
of America"**; published by: Torstar Books, N.Y.;
Editor Henry Commager printed in
YUGOSLAVIA. 1975

THE JAPANESE LANGUAGE, Univ.of Chicago Press
1967; Roy Andrew Miller

NIHONGO, in Deference to Japan, the
Athlane Press,London; Roy Andrew Miller

**THE HISTORY OF THE JAPANESE WRITTEN
LANGUAGE,** by Yaeko Sato Habein Univ. of
Tokyo Press; 1984

ORIGINS OF THE JAPANESE LANGUAGE by Roy
Andrew Miller; Univ. of Washington speeches
from 1977-1978 in Japan.

JAPANS MODERN MYTH - by Roy Andrew Miller
1982; Weatherhill

THE JAPANESE LANGUAGE THROUGH TIME, by
Samuel E. Martin; Yale Univ. Press, New Haven;
1987

CLASSICAL JAPANESE-ENGLISH GRAMMAR DICTIONARY Univ. of Sheffield by Jiri Jelinek; 1976; Sheffield Eng. S10 2TN

READ JAPANESE TODAY- Len Walsh Charles E. Tuttle Co.; 1969 & 1987

AMERICAS FASCINATING INDIAN HERITAGE Readers Digest; 1978, James Maxwell, editor Pleasantville, N.Y.

RAND McNALLY WORLD ATLAS, 1968 edition; (A.Schleiter)

NU SUN by Gunnar Thompson, 1989 edition by Pioneer Publishing Co. 2350 E. Gettysburg Ave. Fresno, CA. 93726

INDIAN PLACE NAMES (Kansas) by Rydjord, D'Arcy McNickle Indian Center Library, Newberry Library, Chicago, Il.

Names of Michigan by Romig

INTRODUCTION TO HISTORICAL LINGUISTICS, by A. Arlotto

FROM THE LAND OF THE SCYTHIANS, Exhibition brochure of RUSSIAN Collection, 1975; sponsored by Metropolitan Museum of Art, and Los Angeles Museum of Art. (Ancient treasures from Museum of USSR—3000 BC to 100 BC.)

MAGYAR EVEZREDEK (ANCIENT HUNGARIANS) by Zajti Ferenc, published in Budapest,1939 in Hungarian language.

LINGUISTIC CONVERGENCE by Ronald Scollon

FRANCE & ENGLAND in N. AMERICA by F. Parkman

ADMIRAL of OCEAN SEAS by Samuel Elliot Morrison

CREDITS and ACKNOWLEDGEMENTS

Among the many people contributing information and critique to this very unique study and bold proposal, I would like to thank the following:

Kiyoshi Koseki; Ceramics engineer, Kokubu, Japan
Shizuko Karasawa; Editor, Yokkaichi, Japan
Marshall Payn; Platt College and Epigraphic Society
Chester Wu; Asiatic tri-lingual, MSME Univ. of Ill; Kyoto.
Masami Kohno; Director, Japan Cultural Institute, San Diego
Vern Cornett; Engineer, Kansas City
Endre Barcoszyk; European linguist and historian, San Francisco
Nobihiro Yoshida; Editor, Japan Petrographic Soc., Kyushu, Japan
Adam Shields; Artist, Santa Paula, Ca.
Mani Boyd; Menominee native speaker, Keshena, Wisconsin
Myles Clowers; San Diego City College; Professor of History
Dr. Tim Guile; Menominee researcher

Also there have been many contributors of resource material, among them G. Koenig, N. Carovich, F.Smithana, J.Kramer, John & Leslie Teller—native language specialists of the Menominee nation, B.Bartlett, H.O.Kraus, Dr. John Accomando(UCLA Romance Language faculty), Dr. J.Niwata, and Dr. F. DelaCotera.

For the beautiful renderings showing Indian Reflections which had to be reproduced in black & white, we are deeply indebted to the artist:

Mr. Adam Shields
1147 Bedford Street
Santa Paula, Ca. 93060

The cover design, by Belling & Bernard, includes a hand-stitched rendition of a native American in ceremonial dress, done by Gail O'Kash.

D. R. Smithana

O R D E R   F O R M

ANASAZI Publishing Group
8190 E. Mira Mesa Blvd. Suite 360
San Diego, Ca. 92126

USA--$9.95
CANADA--$10.95

ORDERED BY

Name		
Company	Division	
Address		
City	State	Zip

Quantity	TITLE	Author	Price	TOTAL
	AMERICA, Land of the Rising Sun	Smithana		
	1-2 books, * Postage & Handling		$2.00	
			Total $	

◆ More than 2 books, $1.50 ea. S&H
☞ WRITE FOR QUANTITY PRICES

☐ Check or M.O. enclosed

☐ P.O. (Appvd accts only)

Signed:_____

title:_____

Published by: ANASAZI Publishing Group
San Diego, CA 92126